THE NEW ECONOMICS OF LIQUIDITY AND FINANCIAL FRICTIONS.

David Adler

CFA Institute
Research
Foundation

Statement of Purpose

The CFA Institute Research Foundation is a not-for-profit organization established to promote the development and dissemination of relevant research for investment practitioners worldwide.

ISBN 978-1-934667-77-4

5 December 2014

Biography

David Adler previously wrote the literature review titled *The New Field of Liquidity and Financial Frictions* for the CFA Institute Research Foundation. He is also the author of *Snap Judgment* (FT Press), which is about behavioral economics, and is co-editor, along with Michael A. Bernstein, of the anthology *Understanding American Economic Decline* (Cambridge University Press). Mr. Adler was a producer of PBS's *NOVA* documentary "Mind over Money," which is about behavioral economics, as well as the documentary "America's Crisis in Healthcare and Retirement," also shown on PBS. He is the moderator of the Bloomberg LiveINSIGHTs conference series and author of related white papers. Mr. Adler has contributed to *Barron's*, *Institutional Investor*, the *New Republic*, and the *Financial Times*.

Contents

CE Qualified Activity · CFA Institute   This publication qualifies for 5 CE credits under the guidelines of the CFA Institute Continuing Education Program.

Foreword

There cannot, in short, be a more insignificant thing, in the economy of society, than money.

—John Stuart Mill, *Principles of Political Economy with Some of Their Applications to Social Philosophy*

Feathers and Bricks

What would you think of a scientific field that assumes away one of the most basic aspects of the natural world that the field hopes to understand? Probably not much. Yet modern macroeconomics, astonishingly, assumes away the existence of money, banking, and the rest of the financial sector. As a consequence, macroeconomists didn't foresee the great crash of 2008–2009 because the crash originated in the financial sector, which, according to their predominant model, didn't exist.

That's not as crazy as it sounds. Newtonian and Einsteinian physics assume that there's no friction. Even Galileo, when he compared the speed of dropped feathers and bricks a half century before Newton, knew to allow for friction and concluded that gravity acted equally on the two objects, the difference in their rate of fall being due entirely to resistance from the atmosphere.

A World without Friction

Why assume away something important, such as friction? Simplifying nature in this way creates a base case from which deviations can be measured and explained. Feathers encounter considerable friction. If we didn't know the rate at which bricks fall, we wouldn't be able to measure the greater impact of friction on feathers. Likewise, the economy is full of frictions: Search and transaction costs prevent markets from being perfect or close to perfect, while decisions are made using incomplete information by people who are less than wholly rational.

Macroeconomics, then, has evolved in a way that tends to set aside such distractions as money and the financial sector because it seeks to explain, in as simple terms as possible, the functioning of the real economy—the economy of factories, trucks, natural resources, labor contracts, patents, and so forth. The financial economy, from this viewpoint, is a sideshow involving claims on the real economy—stocks, bonds, commodity futures contracts—but not the real economic goods themselves.

Is Money a Veil or a Lubricant?

In this sense, "money is a veil," as Arthur Pigou famously said, channeling John Stuart Mill as quoted in the epigraph. (Pigou 1949; Mill 1848, moreover, was channeling David Hume's 1752 essay "Of Money." Money as a veil is a core concept of classical economics, but it has leaked through to Keynesian economics too and is basically correct: Without money and finance, we'd have a barter economy that would suffer from huge friction costs but that would not otherwise be very different.) In other words, the use of money as a medium of exchange obscures the real economic phenomena beneath. If that is the case, let's remove the veil and study the real economy.

But financial institutions and instruments do exist, creating and trading them makes up a significant fraction of total economic activity, and they need to be explained and understood. They are best understood as a form of infrastructure, without which the rest of the economy would struggle to function.

A City without Water

In that sense, financial institutions are like water utilities. If you planned a city without a water utility, you could assume one would spring up to fill the unmet need. But you could make some spectacular mistakes, such as deciding that the ideal place for the city—for other reasons—was on a mountaintop in the arid state of Utah. A water utility will not "spring up" there. Likewise, if farmers need to borrow to plant in the spring so they can harvest in the fall and repay the loans, you could "assume a bank." The need for a bank in such a situation is so obvious that investors would be falling all over each other to establish one.

In a modern economy, which is much more complex than a farming economy, the need for financial institutions is even greater, and the instruments they use include equities, derivatives, and every manner of loan or bond. Yet it's still possible to model the economy without a financial sector, and in order to pierce the monetary veil and see through to the real assets and transactions behind it, macroeconomists have generally done so. For reasons of mathematical tractability, their models—especially the so-called dynamic stochastic general equilibrium (DSGE) models—have staying power.

But having assumed away the financial sector, DSGE models and their kin did not and could not foresee the crash of 2008, nor did they even assess the possibility of such a crash. They could not see that the mechanism that prevents the economy from seizing up because of transaction costs (say, from having to barter) might stop working from time to time and cease to provide capital—or, *in extremis*, cash from ATMs. In the wake of the global financial crisis, it became evident that macroeconomists needed a new kind of economic modeling that took account of the need for liquidity and the existence of financial frictions.

Conventional financial economics, too, has been neglectful of the effects of illiquidity on capital markets and on investor behavior. Most of modern portfolio theory—and most empirical research in finance—assumes that one can buy or sell as much of a security as one wants to at a price close to that of the previous trade. When this condition fails to hold, markets can behave in ways that classic portfolio theory does not predict. By adding illiquidity to the bundle of characteristics or risks that investors must deal with, research in finance moves closer to the real world and becomes more useful.

A New Economics That Addresses Liquidity and Financial Frictions

At these points of inflection, where traditional economics and finance are joined by the study of liquidity and other financial frictions, lie the new frontiers of economics, as described in David Adler's lucid book. In an unexpected marriage of macroeconomics and finance, a group of pioneering researchers is creating a new body of economic theory. This school of thought treats financial frictions, including illiquidity, in the spirit that modern physics embraces when it acknowledges the friction that causes feathers and bricks to fall at different speeds. Adler, a nonfiction author (Adler 2009), reporter, and documentary producer—who has already written a CFA Institute Research Foundation literature review on this topic (Adler 2012)—now turns his attention to explaining, in accessible language and without formulas, both the conceptual foundations and the practical applications of this new turn in economics.

Adler's exploration of the changes in economics wrought by the global financial crisis and stock market crash is much more than a summary of new theories. The research he describes has direct application to public policy. A new word—"macroprudential"—describes policies, practices, and regulations that are intended to protect the financial system and not just a particular financial institution. A deep understanding of the concepts in this book is necessary for deciding what macroprudential policies to implement.

Investors, too, benefit from knowing what policymakers, financial institution executives, and economic researchers are learning about liquidity and financial frictions. By positioning themselves on the frontier of this change in thinking, investors can improve their decisions about what asset mix to hold and what securities to invest in. Because of the many uses to which knowledge about liquidity and financial frictions can be put and because of the luminous manner in which the author makes difficult ideas simple, the CFA Institute Research Foundation is exceptionally pleased to present this book.

Laurence B. Siegel
Gary P. Brinson Director of Research
CFA Institute Research Foundation
September 2014

Prologue

Past is not prologue, either in market performance or in the changing developments of economic theory itself. The present as well as the future seem very different from the era of financial stability enjoyed by the United States and much of the developed world for nearly 60 years after World War II. That period culminated in decades of high growth and low inflation known as the "Great Moderation," which occurred toward the end of the 20th century. Parallel to this trend—and underpinning it, or so many economists believed—were advances in economics. "Macroeconomics in this original sense has succeeded: Its central problem of depression prevention has been solved, for all practical purposes, and has in fact been solved for many decades," said Nobel Laureate Robert Lucas in his 2003 presidential address to the American Economic Association. This apparent stability ended with the 2008–09 financial crash in the United States and the ongoing crisis in the eurozone. The certainties of mainstream theory crashed along with it.

The New Economics of Liquidity and Financial Frictions is a book about a new approach to economics that began emerging after the crash. A friction is an impediment, obstruction, or constraint that prevents markets and economies from working smoothly. This approach to economics is a departure from the frictionless, idealized world of classical economic and financial theory, such as the Arrow–Debreu model of general equilibrium or the capital asset pricing model (CAPM) of Sharpe (1964) and others.[1] Financial frictions—primarily disruptions to credit and lack of liquidity—are a central issue in today's revision of economics, one that economists had previously overlooked or had trouble formally modeling.

Financial friction theory is largely a synthesis of finance and macroeconomics. In terms of research, it is an ongoing story, one with many promising developments. The practical applications are similarly ongoing. In many cases, policy experiments—such as extreme monetary policy or macroprudential policies—as well as efforts to measure systemic risk are in advance of theory; in other cases, the theory is still too stylized to have immediate applications. Overall, financial frictions, both in theory and in practice, are an immensely complex topic.

---

[1]The Arrow–Debreu (1954) model is the mathematical proof of the existence of a competitive equilibrium, given certain frictionless assumptions. The assumptions of the CAPM regarding frictions are further discussed in Chapter 4. (The consumption CAPM and the intertemporal CAPM, where agents derive utility by consuming a single good over time, are general equilibrium asset pricing models.) Its assumptions regarding frictions are further discussed in Chapter 3.

But in other ways, it is a very simple story. The financial crash and its aftermath showed that reality was not very well described by frictionless models. Instead, the crisis provoked a new set of models, one more in keeping with events actually observed. Friction models do not discard the pure theory of neoclassical economics but, rather, build upon it. Friction theory provides a new framework for viewing the economy. The study of frictions also suggests new prescriptions, such as controls on capital inflows.

This book is organized along a recurrent structure. Each chapter describes the reigning pre-crash frictionless economic orthodoxy and then introduces a financial friction and discusses the practical applications of this new theoretical approach. Typically, friction models are too complex to be captured in a single formula. Unlike, say, the CAPM, which can be concisely expressed in one equation, the feedback loops of these models take up pages of equations, which I chose not to include. Therefore, I instead offer a verbal interpretation of the model, emphasizing its key assumptions, construction, conclusions, and limitations—a narrative that often turns out to be more concise than the model's mathematical expression.

The chapters are grouped into broad themes. Chapter 1 describes the failure of macroeconomics to include a financial sector in its models. These models also formally rule out nonlinear dynamics, whereby a small crisis can be amplified into something much worse through the presence of negative feedback loops. These loops—connecting the financial sector and the real economy or occurring within the financial sector itself—can help cause crashes. They turn a small shock into something catastrophic. Under specific circumstances, booms and busts are perhaps endogenous to the financial system itself. Many of these insights were developed first by Irving Fisher and later by Hyman Minsky, though both were ignored by the mainstream until very recently.

The role of credit in booms and busts is further discussed in an interlude section on the "financial cycle." Investors are familiar with the business cycle. Less well-known and more important to explaining financial instability is the insidious credit-driven financial cycle. Peaks in the cycle are associated with an increased likelihood of financial crises.

Chapter 2 looks at frictions in an international economic context. Its surprising policy conclusion is that free capital flows can be very damaging—an insight at odds with the prevailing policy and theory orthodoxy of the pre-crash world. Capital flows and the frictions or "externalities" they create also explain a great deal about the booms and busts of the eurozone peripheral countries.

Chapter 3 applies friction theory to asset pricing. Traditional asset pricing models do not incorporate frictions, such as illiquidity, nor do they even have a role for financial institutions. Newer models incorporate both, leading to new insights about expected returns. Frictions turn out to have profound implications for asset pricing and investing overall, even though they are ignored by standard asset pricing models, such as the CAPM.

Chapter 4 discusses the slippery concepts of systemic risk and macroprudential policy. There is still very limited theory behind both of these buzzwords, but policymakers, nonetheless, are charging ahead to mitigate these risks to the financial sector, using new tools discussed in the book.

Chapter 5 looks back to the recent financial crash to identify several defining, though perhaps overlooked, financial frictions at work and then looks ahead at the future of economics as well as ways to continue to build a stronger financial system.

One theme that appears throughout is a starring role for credit. Credit—including certain types of capital flows—can lead to growth but also to financial instability. Surges in credit are associated with systemic risk. This book exposes the myopia of pre-crash risk management policies that were narrowly focused on value at risk (VaR) or volatility while ignoring growing systemic risks.

Similarly, traditional monetary policy and even monetarism ignored the growth of credit. For too long, central banks, as well as macroeconomists in general, focused almost exclusively on inflation or the business cycle when thinking about monetary policy. Price stability—that is, the lack of inflation—was supposed to ensure financial stability. We now know that this is not the case. The Great Moderation was a period of low inflation and low volatility, but it resulted in a financial crash. It was also a time of a rapid growth in credit and increasing systemic risks.

One conclusion of this book is that economists now have a better understanding of what causes financial crashes as well as how to manage them during their most acute phase. How to recover from them is much less certain and, in some senses, unknown until the results of differing policy efforts are tallied. What is clear is that macroprudential policies will have a much more important role going forward.[2]

An Active Stage of Development

Financial friction theory has not yet reached the stage that Joseph Schumpeter (1954), in his *History of Economic Analysis*, termed a "classical situation"—a settled period, where all the answers are believed to be known. Classical situations are characterized by the following:

> The leading works of which exhibit a large expanse of common ground and suggest a feeling of repose, both of which create, in the superficial observer, an

[2]The term *macroprudential*, like many in this book, lacks an agreed-on, formal definition. The concept of macroprudential policies generally involves policies that improve the stability of the financial system as a whole, as opposed to those that focus solely on individual institutions, which are known as *microprudential* policies.

impression of finality—the finality of a Greek temple that spreads its perfect lines against a cloudless sky. (p. 754)

The periods of John Stuart Mill and, later, Alfred Marshall were classical situations in economics, as were monetarism and the neoclassical synthesis. Certainly, Arrow–Debreu and the macro and finance models in the years leading up to the crash fit this description of a classical situation. Robert Lucas's assessment of the state of macroeconomics, in his previously mentioned 2003 speech, is clearly a classical situation. In all these cases, economics seemed irrefutable and nearly infallible, with all major problems having been solved years before.

This assessment perhaps understates the ongoing tension between Keynesian and neoclassical threads in economic theory between the 1920s and the present—a topic that, unfortunately, I have neither the time nor the space to cover. Although most economists have drawn from each tradition and the two traditions are not mutually exclusive, there are still clear "freshwater" (neoclassical) and "saltwater" (Keynesian) schools of thought, and their adherents disagree on many important topics.[3] For a more detailed discussion, see Krugman (2009).

Financial frictions theory is not in a state of repose or finality. Instead, it is at an earlier stage of development—the more exciting, messy, and innovative stage that precedes a classical situation. As Schumpeter (1954) wrote, "Every classical situation summarizes the work—the really original work—that leads up to it" (p. 48). The study of financial frictions is currently in this period of "really original work"—work that it is still being written, debated, and explored. There are many open questions, both theoretical and practical. This book lays out where there are currently definitive answers—and where there are not—and how policymakers and investors should proceed, often with caution.

One might speculate that when all the answers to improving financial stability are finally known, we will be able to return to the reassuring, albeit boring, era of a classical situation, though not for long: Human ingenuity in creating new crises and problems is probably greater than the expertise that can be developed in advance to prevent them. At least for now, and probably for a long time to come, things are more unsettled than in a classical situation—and, hence, possibly unsettling but also exciting.

---

[3]Freshwater and saltwater refer to US regional concentrations of economists at universities.

Acknowledgments

I would like to thank all those who offered their time and insights during the writing of this book, including Yakov Amihud, Viral Acharya, Robert Barbera, Lasse Pedersen, Paul De Grauwe, Ricardo Delfin, Vanessa Drucker, Mark Gertler, Denis Gromb, Zhiguo He, Olivier Jeanne, Marcin Kacperczyk, Michael Klein, Anton Korinek, Costas Lapavitsas, Enrique Mendoza, Tyler Muir, Yuliy Sannikov, Alan Taylor, William White, and several central bank economists to whom I promised anonymity. All errors are of course mine. I am grateful to the CFA Institute Research Foundation for commissioning this book—particularly the executive director, Bud Haslett, and the director of research, Laurence B. Siegel, for his insights, economic knowledge, and editorial skills.

1. Introducing a Financial Sector into Macro

In the *World Economic Outlook, April 2008*, the International Monetary Fund (IMF) was subdued about the prospects for growth, but it offered no cause for undue alarm or worry: "The US economy will tip into a mild recession in 2008, before starting a modest recovery in 2009" (IMF 2008, p. xv). According to the IMF, other advanced economies were also unlikely to enjoy robust growth, but it did not even forecast a recession for them, merely stating that "activity in the other advanced economies will be sluggish in both 2008 and 2009" (2008, p. 1).

The growth projections for 2008 and 2009 issued in the *World Economic Outlook, April 2008* are reproduced in **Table 1**, with the actual numbers, tallied as of October 2010, shown directly next to them.

The size of the errors remarkable; even the signs associated with each forecast often turned out to be wrong. However, the signs of distress in the world economy in early 2008 were not hard to miss. The United States was in the midst of an almost unprecedented crisis in its financial system: During the period when the *World Economic Outlook, April 2008* was being prepared, Bear Stearns, one of the five major US investment banks, was sold in the face of imminent default. The credit crisis was well underway, with the subprime crisis over a year old.

The IMF was well aware there was an ongoing financial crisis. As the summary of the *World Economic Outlook* noted, this "crisis has led to persistent liquidity shortages, pressure on capital of banks and other financial institutions, increasing credit risks, and sharply falling prices of mortgage-related and other structured securities as well as of equities" (IMF 2008). Despite this evidence of deepening financial turmoil in the United States and the potential for even greater "downside risk," there was no forecast of the severe economic problems in the United States or the world that were soon to arise.

The IMF was not an outlier in terms of its overly optimistic forecasts and mistakes. For instance, the Organisation for Economic Co-Operation and Development (OECD), in a 2014 postmortem about its forecasts during the crisis, acknowledged, "GDP growth was overestimated on average across 2007–12, reflecting not only errors at the height of the financial crisis but also errors in the subsequent recovery" (OECD Economics Department 2014, p. 1).

How did the IMF and other exemplars of sophisticated thinking and modeling in economics get it so wrong? The IMF itself tried to address this question in a self-assessment of its performance leading up to the financial crisis (IMF 2011a). This report, "IMF Performance in the Run-Up to the

Table 1. IMF Growth Projections vs. Actuals for 2008 and 2009

	Projections		Actuals	
	2008	2009	2008	2009
World output	3.7	3.8	2.8	−0.6
Advanced economies	1.3	1.3	0.2	−3.2
United States	0.5	0.6	0.0	−2.6
Euro area	1.4	1.2	0.5	−4.1
Germany	1.4	1.0	1.0	−4.7
France	1.4	1.2	0.1	−2.5
Italy	0.3	0.3	−1.3	−5.0
Spain	1.8	1.7	0.9	−3.7
Japan	1.4	1.5	−1.2	−5.2
United Kingdom	1.6	1.6	−0.1	−4.9
Canada	1.3	1.9	0.5	−2.5
Other advanced economies	3.3	3.4	1.7	−1.2
Newly industrialized Asian economies	4.0	4.4	1.8	−0.9
Emerging and developing economies	6.7	6.6	6.0	2.5
Africa	6.3	6.4	—	—
Central and eastern Europe	4.4	4.3	3.0	−3.6
Commonwealth of Independent States	7.0	6.5	5.3	−6.5
Russia	6.8	6.3	5.2	−7.9
Excluding Russia	7.4	7.0	5.4	−3.2
Developing Asia	8.2	8.4	7.7	6.9
China	9.3	9.5	9.6	9.1
India	7.9	8.0	6.4	5.7
ASEAN-5	5.8	6.0	4.7	1.7
Middle East	6.1	6.1	—	—
Western hemisphere	4.4	3.6	—	—
Brazil	4.8	3.7	5.1	−0.2
Mexico	2.0	2.3	1.5	−6.5
Latin America and the Caribbean	—	—	4.3	−1.7
Middle East and North Africa	—	—	5.0	2.0
Sub-Saharan Africa	6.6	6.7	5.5	2.6

Notes: Projections are as of April 2008. Actuals are as of October 2010. ASEAN-5 represents Indonesia, Malaysia, the Philippines, Thailand, and Vietnam.
Sources: IMF (2008, 2010).

Financial and Economic Crisis," issued by the IMF's Independent Evaluation Office, found that "the key messages that came out of the flagship documents were upbeat" (p. 9), presenting a rosy picture of the economy, with risks facing the financial sector in particular not fully emphasized. Further, any discussion of these risks was undermined by "the accompanying sanguine overall outlook" (p. 1).

The report identified many factors that led to the IMF's failure to fully grapple with the implications of growing financial sector turmoil or to issue clear warnings in its forecasts. It attributes many of these failures to the prevailing "groupthink" and other cognitive biases apparently gripping the institution. Political constraints from member countries, as well as internal governance problems, led to self-censorship and conformity. Additionally, though it is not discussed in the report, perhaps the IMF's forecasting errors also stemmed from the desire not to spread panic. Or maybe it was just bad luck.

But a more likely culprit was not institution specific, lying instead in mainstream economics and models used across the profession. There was a profound intellectual failure in macroeconomics in the years leading up to and during the crisis. The IMF report, to its credit, acknowledges this problem: "The choice of analytical approaches and important knowledge gaps, some of which were shared by the whole profession, also played a role in the failure" (p. 18). This knowledge gap, as the report reveals, stems from the fact that the "*linking of macroeconomic and financial sector analysis* remained inadequate" (p. 18, italics in the original).

The failure to link macro with finance—the "knowledge gap" that the IMF report refers to—can be seen in the most sophisticated macro models in existence, dynamic stochastic general equilibrium (DSGE) models.[4] They were, and still are, widely used in central banks and academia for scenario planning and forecasting. (The 2008 IMF forecast was not produced using a DSGE model, but the bank does use DSGE models to study various "what if" scenarios.)[5] Despite the mathematical complexity of these models, the financial crisis and its aftermath exposed their inadequacy for forecasting or even fully capturing economic reality. Traditional DSGE models suffer from two crippling limitations:

1. In very simple terms, these models lack a financial sector. There are no financial intermediaries.

2. In only slightly less simple terms, these very sophisticated models lack an amplification mechanism, where a small shock could be transmitted into something much more catastrophic.

In DSGE models, the financial sector is merely a "veil" over real activity. The world is one of general equilibrium, with complete markets. There is no room for full-blown financial "frictions" in these models; financial markets are assumed to work perfectly. Hence, there is no need to include or model financial institutions or banks.

---

[4]DSGE models are mathematically complex general equilibrium models that can be used for forecasting. They are often a synthesis of new Keynesian theory and real business cycle theory, and they feature sticky wages. For an overview of the history of these models with an emphasis on how they are used by central banks, see Tovar (2008).

[5]This fact was revealed during a personal conversation with an IMF modeler.

In fact, the real-world puzzle posed by these models, reflecting the Arrow–Debreu frictionless view of the world, is why banks exist at all, except for minor transactional reasons. Given the lack of financial frictions assumed by these models, it is theoretically hard to explain the presence of banks or the size of the financial sector in the outside world.[6]

Secondly, these models do have room for fluctuations in output caused by external shocks, but these fluctuations tend to be small. Internally, there is no amplification mechanism in these models whereby a small shock could lead to a large change in output. They have no fire-sale-generating properties, a case where everyone runs to the exit. A small shock cannot generate a feedback loop that magnifies the problem into something much worse. Instead, in these models, the economy always moves back to normal, with little amplification or persistence of shocks. In essence, bad outcomes are assumed away.

The construction of these models, including the lack of a financial sector, has theoretical justification, however inadequate it turned out to be in the face of the crisis. Underlying the models is not just Arrow–Debreu but also the Modigliani–Miller (1958) theorem and its argument that financial structure is both indeterminate and irrelevant to real economic outcomes. Similarly, real business cycle models and IS–LM[7] models—both of which influenced the vastly more sophisticated DSGE models—assign a role for interest rates but not for credit or financial markets, which, hence, have no influence on the real economy in these models.

Another probable reason DSGE models were constructed along this strange pathway is historical. Prior to the recent financial crisis, the United States experienced no systemic financial crisis during the post–World War II era, the time of these models' construction. (The inflationary crisis of the late 1970s and early 1980s is best described as monetary, not financial.) Economists had no empirical reason to investigate the link between impaired credit markets and the functioning of the real economy, including output and productivity.

Also during this time, although the United States experienced many upturns and downturns, these fluctuations were relatively modest, at least compared with what followed. Stagflation was the major concern until Federal Reserve Chairman Paul Volcker successfully ended it in 1979–1982, and nothing like it happened in the decades that followed. The financial sector certainly was not the driver of these fluctuations.

---

[6]For example, with no financial frictions, companies or governments that want to raise capital might obtain it directly from savers, eliminating intermediaries, such as brokers and money management firms.

[7]The IS–LM (investment saving/liquidity preference money supply) model, perhaps familiar from undergraduate economic textbooks, was developed by John Hicks (1937). It is in the Keynesian tradition but is distinct from Keynes's own work in several respects. For instance, unlike Keynes's own models, it rules out severe crises.

However, outside the United States, the situation was quite different. Other countries experienced numerous financial crises during the post–World War II era, including the Scandinavian banking crisis of the 1990s, "the tequila crisis" in Mexico in 1994, and the Russian and east Asian crises in 1997–1998, just to name a few. The disruption in the real economy caused by these financial crises, as well as the propagation of the initial shock via the financial sector itself, was noticeable, even if in DSGE models the financial sector does not exist. And in many countries that are banking centers, this theoretically nonexistent sector dwarfs the GDP of the country itself. For instance, the ratio of the nonbank financial sector (which is merely a subset of the total finance sector) to GDP is 490% in the Netherlands, 370% in the United Kingdom, 260% in Singapore, and 210% in Switzerland (Financial Stability Board 2012).

Hence, DSGE models arose from a particular historical situation—the post–World War II United States—and apply best to this historical period. This historical and national specificity belies economics' pretense to being a universal social science or, ultimately, a hard science akin to physics. It would be a very strange type of physics and physical laws that holds true only inside certain national borders and only during particular decades.

Reintroducing finance into macro turns out to be extremely challenging from a modeling perspective. Doing so is necessary, however, if economics is going to have anything to say about the real world. Otherwise, economics could become an "empty fortress," heavily defended by models with great internal logic, rigor, and elegance but having no external logic outside of this closed system.

The rest of this chapter—and much of this book—is devoted to chronicling the intellectual efforts of introducing a finance sector into macro and exploring the impact of "frictions" that can result. This chapter in particular focuses on the relationship between the "friction" of an impaired financial sector and its effect on output in a domestic context. Subsequent chapters look at frictions in an international context, as well as how frictions affect asset pricing and create new types of risks that are not yet part of conventional risk measurement practices.

The next section examines historical economists outside the mainstream who were interested in how financial frictions could amplify or even give rise to shocks felt in the real world. These economists took the possibility of a crippled financial sector very seriously. This historical section is followed by a discussion of current attempts to build contemporary macro models that link macro and finance. Such models are very much a work in progress and are incomplete.

These new theories hold great insights for practitioners interested in why financial crises are different from other crises, as well as how to see them coming. The pernicious aftereffects of financial crises that damage the rest of the economy are described in the concluding, empirical section of this chapter.

Background

Irving Fisher's "Debt-Deflation Theory of Great Depressions." The following analysis of a boom and the role leverage plays in it sounds almost as if it were written about the US housing market in the 2000s:

> Over-indebtedness may be started by many causes, of which the most common appears to be new opportunities to invest at a big prospective profit, as compared with ordinary profits.... Easy money is the great cause of over borrowing. When an investor thinks he can make over 100% per annum by borrowing at 6%, he will be tempted to borrow, and to invest or speculate with borrowed money.

The following sentence, however, reveals that we are in fact reading about the 1920s: "This was a prime cause leading to the over-indebtedness of 1929" (Fisher 1933, p. 348).

The Yale University economist Irving Fisher wrote this analysis in his 1933 "creed" (his words), "The Debt-Deflation Theory of Great Depressions." Even more impressive than his description of leverage behind a boom was his analysis of a bust. In the 1933 paper, Fisher dismissed explanations of the causes of the Great Depression that were popular in his day, such as "maladjustment between agricultural and industrial prices, and the discrepancy between saving and investment" (p. 340). Instead, Fisher zeroed in on what he felt was the truly critical factor that explained the severity and persistence of the Depression, an insight that still resonates today:

> In the great booms and depressions, each of the above-named factors has played a subordinate role as compared with two dominant factors, namely *over-indebtedness* to start with and *deflation* following soon after. In short the big bad actors are debt disturbances and price disturbances.... Over-investment and over-speculation are often important; but they would have far less serious results were they not conducted with borrowed money. (p. 341)

Fisher's 1933 paper, therefore, linked together leverage, debt, deflation of financial and real assets, and deleveraging in a downward spiral that results in an economic catastrophe. His basic story was that highly leveraged agents, in order to meet their debt obligations during a downturn, conduct a fire sale of assets, which depresses not just the economy but also nominal prices, leading to an actual *increase* in real debts and an even greater need to liquidate.

The paper had several innovations, often lacking in later literature. Most notable was the role for a negative feedback loop that amplifies an initial shock. As investors find their real debts increasing during a deflationary spiral, they try to sell even more assets, creating additional downward price pressure, and the spiral intensifies. Fisher correctly pointed out that this loop can explain the severity of depressions as well as why the economy does not automatically return to the stable equilibrium presumed by his peers. Fisher even laid out in an appendix of an early work, "Booms and Depressions," and repeated in the 1933 paper the possible sequence of this cycle (see **Exhibit 1**), which is very similar in intuition to the sophisticated, mathematical liquidity theory literature of the 2010s.

Exhibit 1. Irving Fisher's Debt-Deflation Cycle

I.
(7) Mild gloom and shock in confidence
(8) Slightly reduced velocity of circulation
(1) Debt liquidation

II.
(9) Money interest on safe loans falls
(9) But money interest on unsafe loans rises

III.
(2) Distress selling
(7) More gloom
(3) Fall in security prices
(1) More liquidation
(3) Fall in commodity prices

IV.
(9) Real interest rises; real debts increase
(7) More pessimism and distrust
(1) More liquidation
(2) More distress selling
(8) More reduction in velocity

V.
(2) More distress selling
(2) Contraction of deposit currency
(3) Further dollar enlargement

VI.
(4) Reduction in net worth
(4) Increase in bankruptcies
(7) More pessimism and distrust
(8) More slowing in velocity
(1) More liquidation

VII.
(5) Decrease in profits
(5) Increase in losses
(7) Increase in pessimism
(8) Slower velocity
(1) More liquidation
(6) Reduction in volume of stock trading

(continued)

Exhibit 1.   Irving Fisher's Debt-Deflation Cycle (continued)

VIII.

(6) Decrease in construction

(6) Reduction in output

(6) Reduction in trade

(6) Unemployment

(7) More pessimism

IX.

(8) Hoarding

X.

(8) Runs on banks

(8) Banks curtailing loans for self-protection

(8) Banks selling investments

(8) Bank failures

(7) Distrust grows

(8) More hoarding

(1) More liquidation

(2) More distress selling

(3) Further dollar enlargement

Source: Fisher (1933).

Put more formally, Fisher introduced nonlinear dynamics (though he did not use any such term) and amplification mechanisms in the following sense: A shock of small magnitude can lead to changes of much larger magnitude through the feedback loop he described.

Though he did not give the financial sector a starring role in propagating the Great Depression, he did offer an interesting perspective on money, identifying it as more than just a unit of exchange. He pointed out that the debts that investors accrue are nominal, so as prices go down, real debts increase. The intersection with leverage is the key driver in his negative feedback loop. And Fisher also offered a proto-theory of leverage. Easy credit, combined with expectations of further profit, causes investors to borrow more and more.

This picture is reminiscent of the recent US crisis and the leverage-driven real estate boom that preceded it. Even if the economy as a whole did not go into the deflationary loop described by Fisher (perhaps because of aggressive action by the Fed), home prices did, as did many assets held by banks when every bank sold at once.

Fisher's failure, though, at least for economists who followed him, was his lack of formal theory. There is a long way to go from Fisher's verbal descriptions to the macro models of today that contain negative feedback mechanisms. A second problem marring Fisher's reputation, and perhaps influence, was that he was a terrible forecaster.

Fisher had his own quantitative methodology for stock forecasting, based on "popularity."[8] Unfortunately, this approach led him to issue the infamous forecast on 15 October 1929 that stocks had reached "a permanently high plateau."

This forecast was followed by another optimistic forecast on 23 October 1929: "Any fears that the price level of stocks might go down to where it was in 1923 or earlier are not justified by present economic conditions." Then on "Black Thursday," when the market lost 11% of its value at the opening, Fisher said the slump was only "temporary" and the run-up in the market since World War I was justified. Black Friday followed the next day, and Fisher, for once, issued no optimistic forecast.

Part of Fisher's optimism stemmed from his belief in the huge productivity improvements that would ensue from Prohibition, in which he was an adamant believer.[9] He was badly personally affected by the Depression, having "put his money where his mouth was" in terms of heavily investing in the stock market. Even though he was financially ruined, however, he had the intellectual composure to investigate what caused the Depression. He set forth the results of his investigation in his 1933 paper.

Although not widely discussed today, the paper also provided insights about how to end a depression. Whereas most of the debate following the recent Great Recession is about the efficacy of fiscal stimulus versus austerity, with heated and even emotional arguments from both camps, it is safe to say that Fisher would have had none of this. The only way to end a depression, he argued in his 1933 paper, is to directly treat the cause: the debt-deflation loop. Perhaps he was being overoptimistic as usual, but Fisher had a solution: "I would emphasize the important corollary, of the debt-deflation theory, that great depressions are curable and preventable through reflation and stabilization" (Fisher 1933, p. 350).[10]

What Did Keynes Say and When Did He Say It? If Fisher argued that the core of a crisis is declining prices, Keynesian arguments are the opposite: Wages do not drop enough for markets to clear. Stickiness in nominal wages prevents a return to financial stability. Hence, in Keynes's writings or, more precisely, in the IS–LM framework that followed them, the primary friction is one of price. Financial frictions are not central to these arguments at all.

---

[8]For more on Fisher's approach see Dominguez, Fair, and Shapiro (1988).
[9]Fisher was a passionate supporter of Prohibition. He authored the pro-Prohibition tract *Prohibition at Its Worst* (1926).
[10]I am indebted to Enrique Mendoza for his discussions with me about Fisher's views on nonlinearities and crises. For a formalization of some of these insights, see Mendoza (2010).

As Keynes wrote in *The General Theory of Employment, Interest, and Money*, "in fact we must have *some* factor, the value of which in terms of money is, if not fixed, at least sticky" (1936, Chapter 21, Section V). He continued, "Workers are disposed to resist a reduction in their money-rewards" (Chapter 21, Section V). His conclusion was that "apparent unemployment . . . must be due at bottom to a refusal by the unemployed to accept a reward which corresponds to their marginal productivity" (Chapter 2, Section IV).

These statements may seem clear, but what Keynes really meant is the subject of ongoing and charged academic debate—much of it highly esoteric. It is far from clear whether Keynes himself advocated the centrality of wage stickiness to a crisis and to economic instability. According to one camp, a focus on wage stickiness is an excessively narrow reading of Keynes and, if anything, Keynes was mocking this idea in his statements. For instance, Eatwell and Milgate, in their book *The Fall and Rise of Keynesian Economics*, argued that Keynes's theory of unemployment "does not depend on any assumption of wage rigidity" (2011, p. 260). Instead, they claimed that Keynes actually argued that any severe drop in nominal wages would shatter confidence; the stickiness in fact prevents asset prices from falling to zero.

Similarly, macroeconomist Axel Leijonhufvud (1968), in *On Keynesian Economics and the Economics of Keynes*, teased apart differences between what Keynes wrote and the Keynesian economics that came afterwards. Leijonhufvud also questioned the importance of wage stickiness to Keynes's actual arguments: "He realized that if financial markets failed to coordinate investment with saving from full employment income, flexible wages would not bring the economy to full employment" (1968, p. 5).

The debate stems, in part, from the sheer size of the literature labeled "Keynesian" that arose after Keynes and, hence, contains much potential for divergence from purity of the arguments of "the Master." But part of the problem is the lack of clarity in Keynes's own writing. As Eatwell and Milgate admitted, "It is well known that Keynes not infrequently couched general statements . . . in terms that were, at best, somewhat ambiguous" (2011, p. 254).

What is less ambiguous than Keynes's writings is that Keynesian economics after Keynes—namely, the IS–LM framework—deploys price, rather than credit, as its central friction. The IS–LM model depends on stickiness in wages to explain lack of full employment. New Keynesian DSGE models of today, even if they are mathematically much more sophisticated than the IS–LM framework, similarly typically assume sticky prices as a central friction.

What is also not ambiguous is Keynes's lack of an explicit or fully described banking sector in *The General Theory*. This omission haunts even the most ardent of today's Keynesian economists, such as Paul Krugman (2011):

Perhaps the most surprising omission in *The General Theory*—and the one that has so far generated the most soul-searching among those macroeconomists who had not forgotten basic Keynesian concepts—is the book's failure to discuss banking crises. There's basically no financial sector in *The General Theory*. Textbook macroeconomics ever since has more or less discussed money and banking off to the side, giving it no central role in business cycle analysis.

Today, following a deep crisis stemming from a financial collapse, Keynes still has much to say about amplification mechanisms. Whereas most neoclassical models have difficulty explaining the severity of the recent crisis, Keynes at least considered the possibility of "nonlinear" dynamics and continuing instability stemming from an external shock. His writing about animal spirits and financial speculation also contained notions of nonlinearities.

However, a banking crisis and near depression following a boom in leverage is not a classical Keynesian story. Scholars who have devoted their lifetimes to studying Keynes, such as Axel Leijonhufvud, recognize this. They propose looking forward, rather than back toward Keynes, for the answers. They even subtly suggest that if Keynes were alive today, he would be doing the same and working toward new theory.

According to Leijonhufvud (2009), Keynes would not "be happy to see economists get absorbed in scholastic disputes over the economic thought of 70 years ago." Instead, according to Leijonhufvud, "we should learn from Keynes to focus on the macro-problems of our day. Today's problem is the financial crisis.... Neither the standard Keynesian policies of decades past nor the monetary policy doctrine of recent years provides useful solutions. [DSGE] theory is part of the crisis wreckage, but turning to old or to New Keynesian theory will be of little use" (2009).

Minsky's Moment. Hyman Minsky was an economist whose concerns seem much closer than Keynes's to today's problems of a financial crisis followed by a crisis in the real economy. (To be fair to Keynes, Minsky's work is much more recent; he died in 1996.) Minsky was deeply focused on bank balance sheets and changing perceptions of risk.

In Minsky's framework, finance is front and center to a boom and bust. As he wrote, "Capitalism is essentially a financial system, and the peculiar behavior attributes of a capitalist economy center around the impact of finance upon system behavior" (Minsky 1967, p. 33).

The outline of Minsky's story is that of finance-led business cycles. The cycle has three steps, consisting of different debt "units"—hedged, speculative, and Ponzi financing—of increasing riskiness. Hedge units are able to service their debt requirements. Speculative units, in his language, have the cash flow to pay their interest payments but not their principal. Ponzi units do not have enough cash flow for either and are dependent on the rising prices of their underlying assets for their continuing existence. Over time, the economy migrates to increasingly risky financing following this three-step process.

The essence of Minsky's "financial instability hypothesis" is that good times give rise to instability. This cycle is endogenously driven. The growing boom lowers perceptions of risk, and the economy migrates from stable internal financing to speculative and Ponzi financing. Eventually, the system collapses in what later economists have called a "Minsky moment."[11]

Despite Minsky's idiosyncratic language, his financial instability hypothesis rings true in describing many recent booms and busts, such as that of the US housing markets, where financing was often "Ponzi." (Charles Ponzi was known for an investment fraud in the United States in the 1920s, in which early investors were paid with funds raised from later investors, rather than from actual profits.) Barbera (2009) fully explored some of the applications of Minsky's ideas to the crisis and the functioning of the overall economy:

> Minsky's thesis can be explained in two sentences: A long period of healthy growth convinces people to take bigger and bigger risks. When a great many people have made risky bets, small disappointments can have devastating consequences. Mainstream policymakers, economists, and central bankers spent the last 25 years willfully ignoring these two self-evident truths. (Preface, p. xiv)

But one cannot rely on Minsky as the consummate guide to the recent and still ongoing global crisis. Some technical limitations of his work include the facts that his focus was on businesses, not households, and that he wrote for a postwar era of limited capital flows as opposed to the global financial era of today (Mehrling 2011).

A still unresolved question is whether this boom–bust pattern in credit markets is in fact endogenous, as Minsky believed, or whether regulators are still better served looking for external causes and shocks. This debate about the importance of endogenous versus exogenous shocks is still unresolved and is likely to be so for many years to come.

Minsky's ideas about booms and busts, obscure before his death, have migrated to the mainstream. Wall Street analysts today regularly pronounce various market turning points as "Minsky moments." (They seem less aware of his solution for stabilizing the cycle: "Big Government.") But even proponents of Minsky, such as the economic historian Perry Mehrling (2011), have advised caution:

> So we can hardly say "Minsky was right," and stop there. Rather, what Minsky was right about was…the inherent instability of credit. That also is not a place to stop so much as it is a place to start.

---

[11]The phrase was coined by Paul McCulley in 1998.

Financial Frictions and Amplification Models: Contemporary Approaches

First-Generation Models. Contemporary friction models have formalized these "stories" and, in doing so, have integrated some of the intuitions of earlier economists, such as Fisher, into mainstream macroeconomics. In fact, this was the precise motivation for pioneering mainstream work in this area undertaken by Bernanke and Gertler (1989, 1990) and their model of how financial frictions can amplify a shock, known as the "financial accelerator." As Gertler wrote, "The model provides a formal basis for Irving Fisher's 'Debt Deflation' theory of the Great Depression" (1994, p. 10).

Adding financial frictions into modern macro models has been enormously challenging for many technical reasons. For one, it is not easy to marry the broad intuitions of early theorists, such as Fisher or Minsky, to the institutional details of today, including new asset classes and contemporary risk management practices and regulatory approaches. The main challenges are formal: It is very hard to mathematically model a financial sector that endogenously generates booms and busts. In fact, because of the way the models are constructed, it is very hard to introduce a financial sector into DSGE models at all.

The reason is that DSGE models traditionally are composed only of "representative agents." All agents in the models are alike. Adding in a financial sector and financial frictions requires introducing new types of agents: borrowers and lenders (who differ in their characteristics). Without this new type of agent in these models, representative agents would have to borrow and lend to themselves.

One modeling pathway forward has come not from macro but from academic finance—specifically, the "liquidity" literature (discussed later in this book, in Chapter 3). Here, several sophisticated models—those of Brunnermeier and Pedersen (2009) and Gromb and Vayanos (2002)—carve out a unique role for financial intermediaries. Constraints on this sector can amplify initial losses, leading to persistent departures from fundamental values as well as to financial contagions. Modern macro models with a financial sector are formally constructed almost exactly the same way as these liquidity models; only the objectives are different. In macro, a financial friction or disruption to the financial sector leads to persistent downturns in the real economy; in academic financial models, the friction leads to persistent deviations in asset pricing.

In general, the macro literature is focused on the consumer and consumption whereas the finance literature is focused on the investor and asset pricing, but there are many aspects common to both fields. A foundational paper for both is Grossman and Miller (1988), which acknowledged that markets do not consist of only buyers and sellers but also of financial intermediaries, whom they called "market makers." The risk-bearing capacity of market makers is critical for the functioning of the markets they are involved in.

In macro in particular, the first fully articulated "financial friction" macro models are those of Bernanke and Gertler (1989, 1990) and Bernanke, Gertler, and Gilchrist (known as BGG 1996, 1999). The BGG model is one whose influence remains today. The model was created during the height of the dominance of real business cycle theory, which had no room for financial markets, frictions, or money.

The word "accelerator" used in this model was taken from Samuelson's (1939) "multiplier accelerator model" of business cycles.[12] Here, it refers to credit markets' role in accelerating and propagating shocks that affect the real economy. The model moves beyond the comparatively simple world of representative agents to include two types of agents: lenders and borrowers (who can be thought of as entrepreneurs). The central financial friction works through changes in borrowers' net worth. A shock to the economy reduces their net worth. A resulting decline in their creditworthiness increases their cost of financing. With entrepreneurs not able to fund their projects, there is an impact on real output, and a vicious feedback loop ensues, which further lowers net worth. This cycle intensifies, rather than moderates, during a recession because entrepreneurs have lower profits to turn to for self-financing. Hence, the dynamics of the model are nonlinear. BGG are mathematically able to show how credit market conditions can amplify a shock.

Ironically, in the strictest sense, the model still lacks "banks." There are no explicit financial intermediaries. Instead, the amplification effects central to the model involve the actions and constraints of borrowers, rather than banks, which do not formally exist.

Kiyotaki and Moore (1997) developed an equally influential model that similarly incorporates financial frictions, resulting in a feedback loop. The model is complementary to BGG. Here, the financial friction is centered on the plunging value of collateral, called "land" in the model, rather than borrowers and their net worth as in the BGG model. Ironically, much like the BGG model, there are no financial intermediaries in this model. Instead, there are only "farmers" and "gatherers." Land, in addition to being used for production, is the source of collateral for loans. A small shock reduces the value of this collateral, leading to constraints in borrowing and then to a reduction in output, which feeds back into reducing land values, and the loop continues on and on.

Both models, regardless of the way each is specified, convey the same insight: A small shock can be amplified through a negative feedback loop involving plunging collateral/net worth and lower aggregate output and asset prices, leading to a persistent and severe downturn (see **Figure 1**).

---

[12]This is according to a personal conversation with Gertler.

Figure 1.   The Financial Amplifier

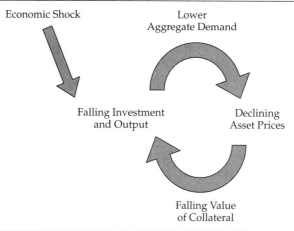

Next-Generation Models. The newest generation of macro models with financial frictions offers several formal innovations absent in the first-generation attempts. These innovations allow the models to more closely replicate and match the market turmoil observed in the recent crisis and the linkages between a financial crisis and a crisis in output.

Today's models are moving forward on two fronts: to explicitly include a financial sector and to use a new type of solution method that does not assume away bad outcomes. Though the resulting models are still highly stylized, they present a world more prone to financial instability than anything conveyed in earlier friction models, such as the BGG and the Kiyotaki and Moore models, to say nothing of DSGE models or the IS–LM framework.

■ *New solution methods.* The previous macro literature, including even the amplification models with frictions of the 1990s, is largely modeled on the economy observed after World War II. In the United States, at least, there were only relatively modest fluctuations in output, and the Fed was able to moderate these fluctuations. Hence, because the fluctuations were small, it was appropriate to study the economy's movements in a very narrow region using a particular type of solution method, known as "log-linearizing around the steady state."

Using this solution method, a stable outcome is mathematically assured; the economy must eventually return to stability. Hence, older macro friction models using this method, such as the BGG and the Kiyotaki and Moore models, show how the economy will eventually be pulled back to stability—the steady state—regardless of some of the amplification effects it faces on the way there. Kiyotaki and Moore acknowledged much of this (in a footnote): "We shall be concerned with characterizing the equilibrium path that converges back to the steady state" (1997, p. 215).

The choice of solution method turns out to be critically important in economic modeling. When economic forecasters say, "Our model shows the economy returning to normal soon"—normal meaning full output or full employment—they may be literally correct. Their *model*, because of its use of the log-linear approximations around a steady state, may indeed show a rapid convergence back to a "normal" steady state because it *assumes* that the economy always returns to such a state. But outside the model and the assumptions in it, there is no guarantee that the fluctuations of the real economy will be as small or predictable or that the economy will return to a normal state.

The severity and persistence of the recent crisis call for a different type of modeling solution, one that does not embed the assumption that the economy will soon return to normal. Rather than log-linear approximations around the steady state, this alternative method is to solve for the full dynamics of the model. Here, the steady state is not assured. Instead, there is a distribution of outcomes, ranging from a normal state to a bad state to a very bad state.

Models using this solution method include those of He and Krishnamurthy (2012, 2013) and Brunnermeier and Sannikov (2014), both of which exhibit nonlinear dynamics. The models show how an economy can be prone to instability. Catastrophes are not assumed away. A large enough shock can take an economy from a normal regime to a crisis regime, akin to an airplane tumbling away from a smooth flight path into an uncontrolled dive. Rather than finding a way back to the steady state, the economy can remain in a crisis state for a long period of time. And in the crisis state, volatility spikes and asset prices become more correlated.

▨ *Model construction: Incorporating a financial sector.* The newest generation of models is also distinct from prior friction models in their setup: They explicitly introduce financial intermediaries. (Older DSGE models, as noted earlier, have no financial intermediaries or large amplification mechanisms at all.) This change in model setup gives rise to new amplification mechanisms in which the financial sector plays a starring role, as was observed in the 2007–09 crisis.

For instance, in He and Krishnamurthy (2013), the main shock is to bank equity. This reduction in a bank's equity reduces its risk-bearing capacity, which can set off numerous feedback loops—mostly involving asset prices—that further weaken balance sheets. The core of the model is an equity price spiral: A decline in equity causes banks to sell assets. This action causes a decline in the price of the asset, leading to a decline in the equity value of the banks still holding the asset. This leads to a decline in investment, which, in turn, affects output and consumption, which sets off further loops that weaken banks.

Hence, though very stylized, the model is able to replicate some of the feedback loops involving risk premiums, asset prices, and the banking sector observed in the recent crisis; banks sold mortgage-backed securities but, in doing so, affected prices, further weakening their balance sheets, which led to more sales. Brunnermeier and Sannikov (2014) have developed a macroeconomic model with a financial sector, with many features similar to those of He and Krishnamurthy's model. (Aside from the macro focus of Brunnermeier and Sannikov's model, the biggest difference in construction between the two models is a technical point: In Brunnermeier and Sannikov's model, the interest rate is exogenous, whereas in He and Krishnamurthy's model, it is endogenous.)

These types of models show just how rapidly macro modeling has developed since the recent financial crisis: Macro modeling now includes (1) an actual financial sector, as opposed to the assumption that banks are merely a veil, and (2) new solution methods that give rise to the huge amplifications and nonlinearities seen in the crisis. These new modeling methods have allowed macro to begin to catch up with real-world events and also to present policy solutions not immediately obvious from less formalized approaches.

Practical and Policy Lessons...and Limitations. Incorporating a financial sector into partial equilibrium models and solving without assuming a quick return to a steady state is a very exciting area of macro-modeling theory. But more important is how these models inform or change our understanding of the real world and how theory and empirical evidence align.

On the policy front, the new macro models are mostly a work in progress, but when they are complete, they will be able to offer quantitative guidance on appropriate regulatory or monetary policies for maintaining stability, as opposed to the politically driven or intuitive approaches policymakers must resort to today. For example, the models could offer precise advice on the optimal setting of countercyclical capital requirements for banks (currently, under Basel III, this is up to the judgment of policymakers, based on some systemic risk measures).

The models also point to superior policy solutions sometimes overlooked in the recent crisis. For example, He and Krishnamurthy's (2013) model can be used to quantitatively evaluate different policies being considered by central banks in response to a financial crisis—lowering interest rates, buying distressed assets, or directly injecting equity capital into financial intermediaries. The authors found that, according to their model, the most effective policy is restoring the equity capital of banks.

Macro models with financial frictions also shed light on why financial crises are so uniquely damaging to the real economy compared with an ordinary recession. In all such models, a small shock is amplified into something much worse, through feedback loops in the financial sector itself and between the financial sector and the real economy. The exact nature of each loop is specified differently in each model: through constraints in the bank balance sheet channel in most recent models or through constraints on firms' balance sheets in earlier models. In all these instances, financing is constrained to the most productive agents in an economy, which, in turn, reduces real output, setting off further feedback effects in the financial sector, and this cycle goes on and on.

At the same time, a close empirical examination of how financial crises affect the real economy also exposes some of the limitations of current theory. Though a financial sector has now been added, there is still a lot missing from current models.

◾ *Empirical evidence: Financial crises vs. ordinary recessions.* One easy way to see how financial crises are uniquely damaging—more so than ordinary recessions—is to compare the 2000 dot-com crash with the 2007 subprime crisis. The tech crash of the early 2000s involved $8 trillion in equity losses. In contrast, the initial subprime mortgage losses in 2007 were only $500 billion.[13] Clearly, the magnitude of these losses is not comparable, but neither was the collateral damage. The tech crash was (briefly) devastating to one industry and its investors. The subprime crisis triggered the Great Recession, which was devastating to the entire US economy and eventually the world.

The distinction between these two episodes is that the dot-com crash was largely a stock market phenomenon whereas the 2007 subprime crisis was an actual crisis of the financial system (because of financial intermediaries' heavy reliance on mortgage-backed securities for use as collateral). The tech crash did not cripple institutional lenders and the broker/dealers of Wall Street, so the damage was contained. In contrast, the subprime crisis was amplified and propagated by the involvement of the financial sector, exactly as macro friction models explain. (For a more detailed description of how the 2007–09 crisis unfolded in the financial sector, see Chapter 5.)

Financial crises are different from ordinary recessions not just in their impact on output but also in their impact on risk premiums, including spreads and volatility. There are significant increases in both during a financial crisis, as well as a marked decline in the value of financial assets in particular. During a conventional recession, there are no comparable changes.

These changes in risk premiums in a financial crisis even overshadow changes stemming from a threat of war or from war itself. The possibility of geopolitical strife, such as the Cuban Missile Crisis, does not automatically translate to an increase in financial risk premiums. Credit spreads remained flat during the Cuban Missile Crisis. Similarly, dividend yields and credit spreads were largely unaffected by the attack on Pearl Harbor (Muir 2014).

Muir (2014), examining war disasters from 1900 onward (using data from Barro[14]), found that wars, on average, led to a cumulative loss of consumption of 30% in the countries examined (which tend to be the winners; he excluded consumption data from countries in which markets shut down altogether). But

---

[13]These numbers are from He and Krishnamurthy (2013).
[14]See http://rbarro.com/data-sets/.

strangely, there was no dramatic change in risk premiums in these countries (see **Figure 2**). This observation is at odds with the predictions of consumption-based asset pricing models that are influential in academia, such as those of Campbell and Cochrane (1999), Lucas (1978), and Breeden (1979)—all of which link consumption and asset returns.

Figure 2. Financial Crises vs. Recessions vs. Wars

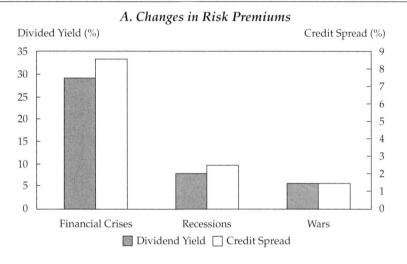

A. Changes in Risk Premiums

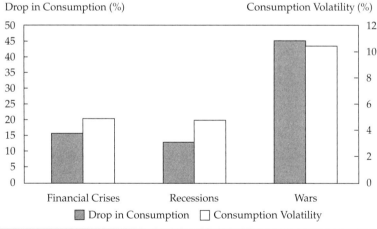

B. Consumption State Variables

Notes: This figure shows Muir's findings on the effects of financial crises, recessions, and wars on risk premiums and consumption. Panel A shows changes in risk premiums, as measured by dividend yields (left axis) and credit spreads (right axis). Panel B plots consumption state variables argued to capture variation in risk premiums: the peak-to-trough decline in consumption (left axis) and consumption volatility (right axis).

Source: Muir (2014, p. 32).

Muir found that "drops in consumption and consumption volatility are similar across financial crises and recessions and are largest during wars, so consumption-based models cannot explain this variation" (2014, abstract). The largest spikes in spreads occur during a financial crisis, a result consistent with the idea that financial crises are uniquely damaging. The amplification effects and feedback loops characteristic of these crises can make them even more damaging to financial assets than a war.

■ *Limitations.* One limitation of financial friction theory revealed by empirical evidence is that the impact on the real economy of a financial crisis is even *worse* than many models predict. Financial crises leave severe declines in output and employment in their wake, as documented, for example, by Reinhart and Rogoff (2009) in their book *This Time is Different.* But these dramatic drops in output are larger than those mechanically generated by models where agents self-insure against financial crises through savings. This is the critique of Kocherlakota, who wrote that "if agents have a lot of savings, then such a shock would lead to just a slight dip in output" (2000, p. 9).

Not only are these economic crises worse than models mechanically anticipate, but they also last longer. Most highly stylized models, of course, do not have a precise time limit for how long an economic downturn should last after a financial shock. But the intuition behind these models is that once the frictions inside the financial sector itself have been corrected and credit is fully restored, the real economy should recover as well. Instead, in the United States, credit markets returned to something close to normal functioning well in advance of the real economy (Hall 2010).

The reason for this unexplained lag effect might be that a financial crisis unleashes additional "frictions," broadly defined, in the real sector that are not captured in current financial friction models. These models focus almost exclusively on credit markets, bank balance sheets, and, sometimes, firms' balance sheets. Households and their balance sheets are largely overlooked. Nonetheless, households can be important in amplifying and propagating a crisis.

Mian and Sufi (2009, 2010, 2014) have taken this argument even further. According to them, the collapse in housing wealth and the increase in household debt—not the financial sector—were the main drivers of the 2007–09 crisis. They provided empirical evidence at a county level to support their thesis, which also heavily draws on concerns about inequality as a key component of this episode. They found that the 2007–09 crisis did not affect all households equally: Poor and highly leveraged households were uniquely hit and experienced the most extreme decline in consumption. This extreme decline in consumption accounts for the severity and persistence of the Great Recession, according to Mian and Sufi.

One insight is that a decline in house prices meant that homeowners who were highly leveraged (with a high loan-to-value ratio) saw their equity wiped out. Their credit scores were also affected by the decline. These problems led to a shock to consumption. An important contribution of Mian and Sufi's work is that it showed that marginal propensity to consume (MPC) is dependent on leverage and income. According to these researchers, overall, the Great Recession is thus largely a story about a collapse in demand driven by the loss of housing wealth of these high-MPC households. Mian and Sufi's (2014) policy solution is debt forgiveness of these households and new types of consumer debt contracts: "The dramatic loss in wealth of indebted home owners is the key driver of severe recessions. Saving the banks will not save the economy. Instead, bolstering the economy by attacking the levered-losses problem directly would save the banks."

Missing from this solution and analysis is a full acknowledgement of the government housing policies that encouraged highly leveraged home purchases in the first place. Whereas margin requirements for stock purchases are tightly regulated, when it came to home purchases, regulator and lender concerns about the buying of homes on margin and overall household leverage seemed to fly out the window.[15]

Moreover, these are nonrecourse loans; homeowners can walk away from them. Hence, there is a floor to these debts, limiting the potential damage from Irving Fisher–style debt-deflation loops. Overall, focusing on housing wealth and consumption is not a satisfactory explanation of the crisis. It can probably explain why in Merced County, California, which ranked in the top 10 nationally for subprime loans, the fall in home prices led to a fall in spending of 30%. It cannot explain why in New York City all five of the major broker/dealers ceased to exist as such. It also cannot explain why interbank markets and huge credit markets, such as repo and asset-backed commercial paper, froze or why the financial crisis eventually rippled from the United States to Europe.

In other words, the crisis was more than just a drop in consumption among highly leveraged subprime borrowers, concentrated in specific afflicted US counties. It was a global *financial* crisis, which explains its amplification effects and virulence, exactly as mapped out by macro-finance models.

An understanding of the role of the household sector in the crisis, however, is still critically important. Highly leveraged households, akin to banks, face their own constraints and possibility of deleveraging. Business and employment relationships can be destroyed and can be slow to return, even if credit does. These frictions can all amplify and propagate a crisis but are not formally

---

[15]See Morgenson and Rosner (2011) for a full description of mortgage-lending policies and practices in the United States preceding the crisis.

captured in most current macro-finance models. Overall, interactions between the "real" economy and the financial sector need further modeling and clarity.

There is a lot still missing from current models: household balance sheets, public finance, a role for regulation. The negative feedback loops between a banking crisis and a sovereign debt crisis, key to the dynamics of the events in the eurozone, are not a focus of current models, nor are the problems presented by debt overhang.[16] Nor can most current models replicate a Minsky-type endogenous credit boom that gives rise to a bust; instead, in these models, the shock is external in origin and is amplified by the financial sector. The "missing" list is a long one.

Part of the reason for this oversight in current models is formal in nature. It is hard to capture banks, firms, households, and sovereigns in a single model that does not end up being a kitchen sink model that explains everything and nothing. Finding ways to incisively model the interactions between these sectors and to fully understand what is going on inside households and firms during a financial crisis remains an ongoing, unsolved challenge for friction modeling.

Overall, despite these limitations, friction modelers have rapidly made progress in incorporating a financial sector into macro models. These new models help explain why financial crises are so virulent and damaging.

The next chapter of this book looks at the implications of financial frictions in an international context. Friction theory overturns the conventional wisdom on many fronts and suggests new policy ideas. But first, I will explore the little-known credit cycle and its possible role in booms and busts. This cycle exposes some of the limitations of monetarism and the monetarist view.

The Financial Cycle

Investors are familiar with the concept of a business cycle. This cycle has been a focus of macroeconomic theory and research as well as central bank concern. Less well-known to investors and ignored by macroeconomists, at least until very recently, is the idea of a financial cycle. The financial cycle, sometimes called the *credit cycle*, consists of slow-moving credit booms and busts. Peaks in the cycle are associated with banking crises. Research into the financial cycle has been one of the greatest contributions of recent financial frictions work and has led to the development of new measures of systemic risk.

The concept of a cycle, or periodicity, in economics has a slightly different meaning from that in everyday usage. It implies mean reversion, but not following a predictable pattern or over a precise time period. Despite this caveat, the basic contours of the financial cycle in comparison to the

---

[16]The problem of "debt overhang" and policies for the recovery phase of a financial crisis are further discussed in Chapter 5.

business cycle are clear: It is of much lower frequency and of higher amplitude. Business cycles are more short term, with fluctuations of up to 8 years, whereas the financial cycle is much longer, with fluctuations from 8 years to 30 years (Borio 2012).

Research into the financial cycle is highly empirical, attempting to map out its contours and track its effects and its association with financial instability. One key finding is that the financial cycle moves independently from money aggregates, such as M1 or M2. With credit and money decoupled, the credit cycle reveals that the monetarist view of the world is incomplete, even blinkered. Another finding is that the financial cycle is largely independent from the business cycle—except when distress arising from the collapse of the financial cycle causes the business cycle to tumble. Further, equity performance is more closely related to the business cycle than to the financial cycle.

The idea of a financial cycle has gained new research prominence since the crash, particularly because it is a good indicator of financial vulnerabilities not captured by conventional risk metrics.

Features of the Financial Cycle

The concept of a "financial cycle" is not new. Minsky (1982) and Kindleberger (2000) emphasized the role of credit conditions in creating macroeconomic shocks. It also has similarities to Fisher's idea of a leverage boom followed by a debt-deflation cycle and, more closely, to the Austrian school of Hayek and von Mises, with its focus on bank credit–fueled booms and resulting overinvestment. Hence, the idea of a financial cycle is in many senses older than theories of the business cycle that rose to prominence in mainstream economics in the 1990s.

Neither Minsky nor Kindleberger, however, were mainstream economists. The post–World War II mainstream, as discussed previously, largely dismissed the importance of credit.

What is new today is the focus on the credit cycle by mainstream economists. This has been accompanied by efforts to integrate the cycle into mainstream theory and even more so by empirical work to measure the cycle. However, the current generation of macro friction models described previously still do not map precisely to the idea of the financial cycle; they have a different focus—the dynamics of a financial crash and how a small shock can be amplified by the financial sector, rather than endogenous credit booms and how they can lead to busts. Put another way, current macro friction models mostly focus on the mechanisms of a financial crash, rather than on the entire life cycle of a financial cycle, including the building up of credit.

Much of the research into the financial cycle was pioneered by the economists Borio and White of the Bank for International Settlements (BIS) in the years leading up to the crash, with widespread involvement by other researchers subsequent to the crash, including Claessens, Kose, and Terrones (2011); Schularick and Taylor (2009); Drehmann, Borio, and Tsatsaronis (2012); and Borio and Drehmann (2009).

Like many strands of financial friction theory, the financial cycle lacks a consensus definition. Nor is there a consensus on how to precisely measure the cycle. In general, it is measured by the ratio of credit aggregates to GDP, but there are different empirical approaches as to what credit aggregates to include.

The BIS, for example, uses residential property prices, credit, and the overall ratio of credit to GPD in its calculation of the cycle, which also relies on frequency-based filters for analysis. (The BIS excludes equity prices and aggregate asset prices because of their short-term volatility.)[17] Therefore, the financial cycle, as constructed by BIS researchers, consists of credit and property prices, which tend to co-move, making the cycle subject to pronounced spikes.

The distinctive feature of the resulting cycle is that it is different from the business cycle as shown in **Figure 3**; it is longer and has a greater amplitude. Downturns in the financial cycle are more drawn out and severe than those in the business cycle. Financial cycles contract over several years, unlike the downturns of a year or so seen in conventional business cycle recessions, at least in those that do not coincide with financial cycle downturns. Moreover, the financial cycle has become increasingly pronounced in the United States since the 1980s.

Another approach to measuring the financial cycle, with slightly different inputs, has been taken by the economic historian Alan Taylor (Taylor 2012; Schularick and Taylor 2009). In contrast to simply measuring the relationship between credit and output in a single economy, Taylor examines these relationships in 14 developed countries, using a dataset reaching all the way back to 1870 and ending in 2008. He also looks at money, here defined as M1. Taylor uses two distinct measures of credit: bank loans and bank assets. Bank loans are loans to domestic households and corporations. Bank assets are year-end balance sheets. His measures of credit are, therefore, narrower than those of BIS researchers in that he does not include property prices. Finally, he excludes shadow banks from his definition of "banks," so he understates this credit aggregate.

---

[17]The financial cycle measures deviations in long-term credit-to-GDP trends, which is called the "credit-to-GDP gap." Calculating the size of this gap requires estimating macroeconomic variables, which can be subject to frequent revisions. Chapter 4 addresses the problem this poses for using the credit-to-GDP gap as a warning for growing systemic risk and as a guide for policy.

Figure 3.   The Financial and Business Cycles in the United States

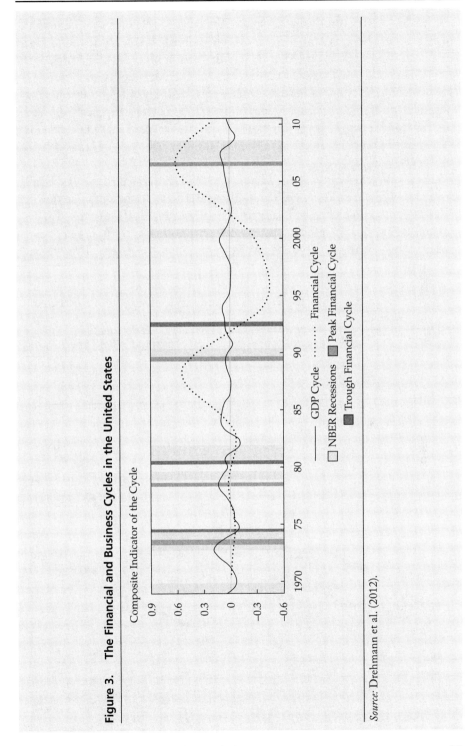

Source: Drehmann et al. (2012).

Taylor's (2012) and Schularick and Taylor's (2009) conclusion, like that of BIS researchers, is that there is evidence of a financial cycle—one that has intensified since World War II. Credit growth precedes and anticipates financial crises, which Taylor characterizes as "credit booms gone wrong." Historically, monetary policy has not been particularly effective at restoring output after financial crashes. Most importantly, Taylor's approach allowed him to tease apart money (M2) from credit. The revolutionary takeaway is that money and bank assets have decoupled after World War II, as shown in **Figure 4**.

Before World War II, money, bank assets/GDP, and bank loans/GDP all moved roughly in tandem. Following the war, the relationship broke down. Credit—both bank loans and bank assets—has dramatically expanded. This is the case not just in a few countries caught up in the crash: Taylor found it across his entire sample of 14 Western nations. It is essentially a global phenomenon.

The monetarist view of the world, focused on money, does not capture this increase in the credit-to-GDP ratio and gives an incomplete picture of

Figure 4. The Decoupling of Money and Credit: Aggregates Relative to GDP

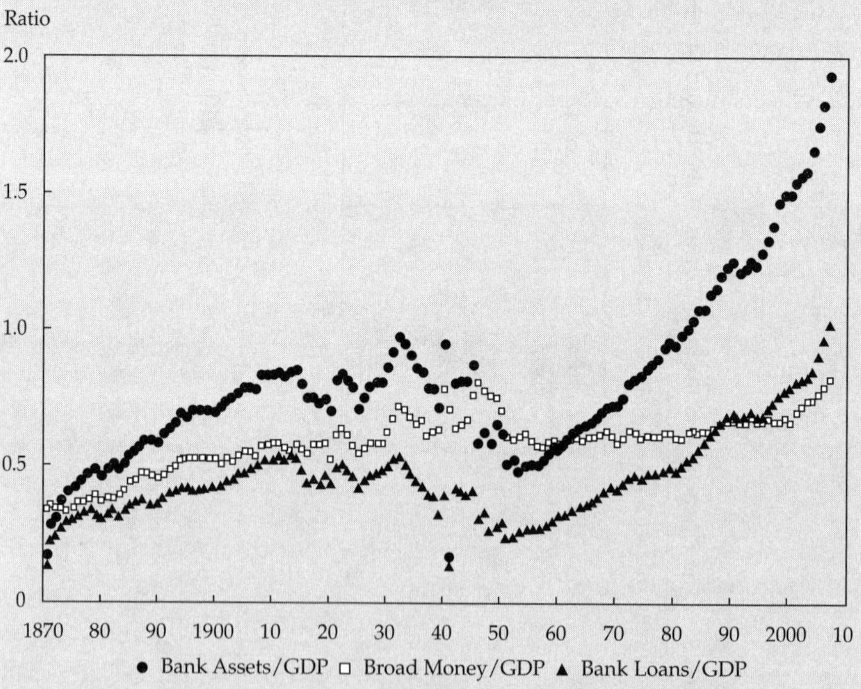

Source: Schularick and Taylor (2009).

contemporary economic mechanisms. Central banks' main focus on inflation misses the growth of credit, which might, in fact, be more central to financial crises than money itself.

Drivers of the Financial Cycle

What causes the financial cycle to fluctuate as well as what has driven the increase in leverage since World War II is not fully understood. Nonetheless, there are several likely suspects.

First, an upswing in the financial cycle coincides with financial liberalization. The mid-1980s marked the beginning of the recent financial cycle and a period of financial deregulation and liberalization. Monetary policy during this period was tightly focused on inflation, rather than on containing growing credit booms.

Loose monetary policy is also associated with an upswing in the financial cycle. However, the link between monetary regimes and the credit cycle is inexact and still unclear (Aikman, Haldane, and Nelson 2010).

More subtly, the growth of the financial cycle probably results from an interplay of factors: ease of funding, ease of regulatory constraints, growth in asset prices, and changing perceptions of risk.

One story of how the credit cycle might unfold goes as follows. During a boom, volatility typically is low and spreads are narrow. Banks, managing their balance sheets using VaR metrics, can increase the size of their balance sheets during these periods. This creates the conditions for a positive feedback loop. As banks expand their balance sheets, the prices of assets held by them increase because there is greater demand for these assets. This increase in prices means banks' balance sheets are stronger still, so they can buy even more assets and do so in a loop that continues on and on. Banks cannot increase their leverage infinitely; the process has to stop someday. Eventually, there is a bust and the whole loop goes into reverse.[18]

Therefore, according to this story, risk measures used by institutional investors, such as VaR or the CBOE Volatility Index (VIX), play a contributing role in the fluctuations of the cycle even though they in no way measure the risks posed by the cycle itself. When perceived risks are low, as measured by VaR, banks expand their balance sheets. This explanation of the growth of the cycle is consistent with the Minsky-like notion that in good times, the price of risk is very low, which leads banks to take on more risks, ultimately creating the seeds of a crisis. Or as Minsky pithily put it, "Stability is destabilizing."

---

[18]For a series of highly technical papers modeling this interplay in great detail with a focus on VaR, see Adrian and Shin (2013); Adrian, Colla, and Shin (2012); Adrian and Boyarchenko (2013).

Containing the Financial Cycle

How should the financial cycle be contained? Should the financial cycle be contained? These questions are still open, given how little is known about the financial cycle. But it is an empirical fact that peaks in the financial cycle are associated with financial crises; ample evidence documents this relationship (Borio 2012; Drehmann et al. 2012).

However, there is still little or no *theory* to fully explain the relationship between the financial cycle and financial instability; there is only the intuition that credit booms are ultimately unsustainable and prone to crashes. Nor is it currently possible to identify turning points in the financial cycle that are indicative of an immediate crash; the financial cycle is very slow moving and is calculated using macro data that take a long time to collect and are subject to frequent revisions.

A key insight of the financial cycle is that there is some sort of tradeoff between credit growth and financial stability. There might be an ideal point in the cycle where the economy should be located, a point that yields sufficient credit growth to foster economic growth but is safely removed from the credit extremes that result in a bust. But for now, no one can identify with any certainty this optimal point. Analysis of the financial cycle is still too preliminary.

Despite these conceptual weaknesses, the financial cycle is critically important on several fronts. Its existence shows that policymakers and investors should focus on credit booms, rather than on just money supply or inflation, when considering looming macroeconomic threats. Moreover, conventional risk metrics, such as VaR or the VIX, in no way capture the risks posed by the cycle and arguably contribute to it if they lead to procyclical expansion of bank balance sheets. Perhaps the key argument for taking the existence of the financial cycle seriously is that the Basel III framework does. Basel III assigns a measure of systemic risk related to the financial cycle as a guide for the setting of countercyclical capital buffers. This measure is discussed further in Chapter 4.

2. Financial Frictions in an International Context: Rethinking the Benefits of Capital Flows

> What used to be heresy is now endorsed as orthodox.
>
> —John Maynard Keynes

Chapter 1 focused on financial frictions in a "closed," domestic economy, with no room for changes in the exchange rate. In the current chapter, the analysis of frictions and their amplification mechanisms is extended to an international context—that is, an "open" economy. This extension points to new sources of booms and busts and raises concerns about the benefits of free capital flows. (Only a few years ago, it was considered heretical to question the advantages of free capital flows.) This new analysis also suggests a policy solution: imposing capital controls to improve overall financial stability.

What is more surprising, and perhaps even counterintuitive, is that the controls that are arguably beneficial are targeted at capital inflows rather than outflows. These seemingly unconventional policy ideas are becoming mainstream, with policymakers increasingly moving away from capital account liberalization. As the International Monetary Fund simply stated in a policy document about managing capital flows, "Capital controls were not seen as part of the policy toolkit, now they are" (IMF 2011b, p. 1).

Therefore, understanding frictions in an international context is useful for many reasons. It offers new insights about the origin of financial crises. It highlights the fact that there is a tradeoff between financial stability and rapid economic growth based on surges in credit. Also, it illustrates how theory can rapidly change once frictions are incorporated into models, leading to conclusions at odds with the prevailing wisdom of only a few years ago.

However, the new theory on capital flows is at odds with empirical literature. Capital controls make sense in theory, but they have been less effective in practice in most instances. Capital controls are, therefore, also an interesting case study of divergence between theory and practice when it comes to financial frictions.

Changing Orthodoxies

Capital inflows have many obvious advantages: They bring capital to countries that need it, resulting in improved returns for investors and improved growth for capital-starved emerging economies. Such investments also help integrate these countries into the global economy, enhancing their level of development. However, this view of the benefits of capital account liberalization and the freeing up of capital flows is no longer dominant, at least at the upper reaches of economic theory and policy. It has been replaced by a more nuanced, or even negative, view of capital account liberalization that takes into account capital flows' potential for setting off booms and Fisher-type debt-deflation busts.

The changing orthodoxy can be seen most clearly in the changing policy positions of the IMF, which might be considered the "gold standard" of conventional economic policy wisdom.[19]

For instance, in 1997, the dominant view was that capital account liberalization was almost entirely beneficial. In a speech that year, Stanley Fischer, then first deputy managing director of the IMF, argued in favor of amending the IMF's Articles of Agreement to promote capital account liberalization. The IMF's original articles already called for current account convertibility and trade liberalization. Fischer's rationale for extending this mandate to include capital account liberalization was straightforward: Most advanced economies at that time had open capital accounts, and he argued that this liberalization was an inevitable step of development toward becoming an advanced economy. According to Fischer, "Free capital movements facilitate an efficient global allocation of savings and help channel resources into their most productive uses, thus increasing economic growth and welfare" (1998, p. 4).

Fischer did note that there could be risks associated with inflows: Countries might be subjected to swings in market sentiment, and "markets are not always right" (1998, p. 3). These risks included the possibility of sudden and destabilizing outflows. However, this vulnerability was more than offset by the discipline supplied by markets. In sum, it was hard to see, on balance, how capital account liberalization could be a bad thing: Capital inflows reduced the cost of capital, helped fund needed development in emerging economies, and better integrated these countries into the world financial system.

The IMF's original Articles of Agreement, which arose from the Bretton Woods Conference in 1944, did allow countries to use capital controls. This position reflected the reigning Keynesian wisdom of that time. Interestingly, Fischer's call for a formal amendment was rejected, in part because of the

---

[19]"Gold standard" has different meanings in everyday use (the best or definitive) and economics (a monetary system based on gold), and this latter definition does not necessarily have the same positive connotations. For instance, Keynes called the gold standard a "barbarous relic." The ambivalence I am trying to convey is that the IMF, once very important in economic research, fell behind in the years leading up to the crash. Under the research direction of Jonathan Ostry and Olivier Blanchard, however, the IMF once again represents the gold standard (in the vernacular, rather than economic, meaning of the word) of contemporary economic thought and research.

still-lingering aftereffects of the East Asian financial crisis. However, despite this rejection, and even with capital controls still enshrined in the Articles of Agreement, the fund continued to pursue a *de facto* liberalization of capital controls at the time of Fischer's paper (Gallagher 2012).

Contrast this 1998 position with the prevailing wisdom of the International Monetary Fund in 2012, as seen in "The Liberalization and Management of Capital Flows: An Institutional View" (IMF 2012). The highly formal "institutional view" of the IMF acknowledged that capital inflows can have benefits, but "at the same time, capital flows also carry risks, which can be magnified by gaps in countries' financial and institutional infrastructure" (2012, p. 1). Though the "institutional view" is immensely guarded, a change in recommended policy is unmistakable. According to the IMF, "in certain circumstances, capital flow management measures can be useful" (2012, p. 2).

The use of neutral language—"capital flow management" instead of "capital controls"—does not hide the fact that the IMF's position today is radically different. This new position may in part simply reflect the post-crisis Zeitgeist that favors a retreat from economic liberalization and a warm embrace of increased regulation and restrictions. But it might also stem from advances in economics and the development of new theoretical financial friction models that identify the possibility of destructive externalities associated with the free flow of capital.

Stanley Fischer himself foresaw the need for a better theoretical understanding of capital flows at the time he wrote his essay, referencing weakness in the prevailing theory at that time. Although he did not precisely anticipate what shape the new economics of capital controls would take, he did note that

> the difference between the analytic understanding of capital versus current account restrictions is striking. The economics profession knows a great deal about current account liberalization, its desirability, and effective ways of liberalizing. It knows far less about capital account liberalization. (Fischer 1998, p. 8)

Capital Controls: Theoretical Foundations

Discussion of capital controls focuses on two mostly distinct issues: (1) monetary autonomy and (2) newer prudential measures designed to ward off booms and busts and exchange rate appreciation.

The role of controls in creating monetary autonomy comes from an older strand of literature and policy. The foundational concept is the "impossible trilemma," sometimes called the "impossible trinity."[20] It holds that economic policymakers can choose only two out of the following three options: free

---

[20]See DeRosa (2009).

capital flows, a fixed exchange rate, and free monetary autonomy in terms of control over the interest rate. Governments have to relinquish control of one option.[21]

The Mundell–Fleming model of the "impossible trilemma" was developed in the 1960s. This model is largely an extension of Keynesian economics and the IS–LM model to an open economy (where borrowing could be conducted in a foreign currency). The model allowed policymakers to analyze monetary policy and fiscal policy in an open economy and to understand these policies' effects on exchange rates and aggregate demand. The major insight of the model—the impossible trilemma—is for the most part not in dispute and remains a rough guide for policy options.[22] In practical terms, one implication of the trilemma is that a capital inflow combined with a fixed exchange rate is tantamount to a reduction in a country's real interest rate. Capital inflows reduce the cost of borrowing.

Current thinking and arguments about capital controls arise mostly from a different strand of the international economics literature. Unlike Mundell's (1961) models, this strand is more concerned with financial stability and currency crises. The focus is on policies to mitigate these crises or even avoid them altogether before they arise. The foundational, or "first-generation," papers are Krugman (1979) and Flood and Garber (1984). In this model, governments attempt to maintain fixed exchange rates but face budget deficits. The government runs out of reserves, speculative attacks ensue, and the currency collapses. This model described and anticipated various Latin American crises of the 1970s and 1980s.

The second-generation models include that of Obstfeld (1994). In this model, governments wish to pursue an expansionary monetary policy at the expense of a fixed exchange rate. Speculators, sensing that the government is unable or unwilling to defend its currency, make a run on it. This model described investor runs on the British pound in the 1990s.

In all these first- and second-generation models, capital flows are not center stage; fixed exchange rates or faulty domestic policies, rather than free capital inflows, are the culprit for the ensuing crisis. Early third-generation models, such as that described in Calvo (1998), consider the dangers stemming from

---

[21]The intuition behind the trilemma is easy to understand. Suppose a country has a fixed exchange rate and free flows of capital. If it attempted to move its interest rate down, for example, investors would leave for a currency with a higher interest rate, which, in turn, would affect the exchange rate. A fixed exchange rate would no longer be tenable. Closed capital markets, however, would allow the country to retain stability in its exchange rate. But under the original setup of fixed exchange rates and fully open capital markets, the country would have to give up monetary autonomy.

[22]The dilemma was recently challenged by Hélène Rey (2013), who argued that "the global financial cycle has transformed the well-known trilemma into a 'dilemma.' Independent monetary policies are possible if and only if the capital account is managed directly or indirectly" (2013).

capital flows, particularly the problem presented by a sudden stop in inflows. However, Calvo did not provide a detailed description of the mechanisms involved. His model itself stops short of considering the negative feedback loop that ensues from a stop and, hence, the full scope of negative externalities posed by flows.[23]

Current Models

The modern view of international financial crises builds on these models in an effort to understand the role capital flows play in producing financial instability; the policy conclusion is a need for capital controls for macroprudential reasons.

Contemporary third-generation models emphasize constraints in credit markets and other financial frictions that can give rise to and amplify international financial crises, leading to Fisher-type debt-deflation loops. Formally, these models are almost exactly the same as the amplification models described in Chapter 1; only here, they are applied to an open economy, where the economy can borrow abroad—until it hits a collateral constraint. And the underlying driver of much of this instability is free flows of capital, which impose externalities on the rest of the economy.

Leading papers in this area are Korinek (2010, 2011a, 2011b); Jeanne and Korinek (2013); and Korinek and Mendoza (2013). The basic setup for these models is to assume that a country borrows in a foreign currency. During a nascent boom, the country experiences inflows, which lead to an appreciation of exchange rates and the value of assets. These assets, such as real estate, can, in turn, be used as collateral to finance more borrowing. This situation sets off additional positive feedback loops, with aggregate demand, exchange rates, and asset prices all rising together, driven by further capital inflows.

But then there is a reversal or shock, perhaps external in origin, and capital flows out. Asset prices, exchange rates, and output all decline, amplifying the original shock. With the value of collateral decreasing, it becomes harder for the country to borrow. The foreign lender asks to be repaid, and everyone is forced to sell. The same sort of vicious Fisher-type debt-deflation dynamics as exist in a large or closed economy ensue, with the additional complication that the exchange rate is collapsing, as illustrated in **Figure 5**. Eventually, the country hits a collateral constraint and loses access to foreign credit markets altogether.

This scenario is a departure from the intuitive, as well as textbook, idea that depreciating exchange rates should stabilize a depressed economy. A decline in the exchange rate should increase competitiveness and, ultimately, growth. But this conclusion rests on the rarely articulated assumption that credit markets are

---

[23]For a full history of the development of first-, second-, and third-generation models, see Korinek (2011a).

Figure 5.   Financial Amplification Effects in an International Context

Capital Outflows

Declining Collateral

Falling Exchange Rates

Source: Korinek (2010).

complete and there are no frictions, which is not the case in this scenario. Here, in contrast, as prices and exchange rates fall, so does the value of collateral. The creditworthiness of the borrowing country deteriorates. Worsening balance sheets amplify these effects as real debt, as measured in a foreign currency, increases. The country faces a binding collateral constraint and can no longer borrow its way back to economic health.

The main driver of these amplification mechanisms is capital inflows. Their impact comes primarily through a price externality. Inflows drive up the exchange rates and asset prices during the boom, and outflows do the opposite during the bust. Individual borrowers do not internalize the effects their actions are having on the market as a whole—such as during a fire sale, when everyone is selling at once and prices collapse. Their actions are in their own interest but cause "pollution" (i.e., they affect the exchange rate and overall economy).

The efficient solution from the economics of pollution is to have agents internalize their externalities via a Pigovian tax.[24] Capital controls are the Pigovian tax in this context. They improve the public good, which in this case is improved macroeconomic stability.

This "tax," in the form of controls on capital inflows, is in a sense a variant or special case of Tobin's proposed tax on foreign financial transactions. Tobin called for a small tax on foreign exchange transactions in order "to throw some sand in the wheels of our excessively efficient international money markets"

---

[24]A Pigovian (sometimes spelled "Pigouvian") tax, named after the British economist Arthur Pigou (1877–1959), is a tax on activities that create negative externalities, which thereby reduces them. A pollution tax is the most common example. A Pigovian tax on polluters internalizes the cost of their activity and reduces pollution.

(1978, p. 158). Tobin's specific objective was to reduce currency speculation while providing more autonomy for monetary policy in smaller countries.

Capital controls, however, are not merely sand designed to slow down the wheels of international finance. Instead, there is a clear theoretical foundation for why policymakers should intervene: to reduce externalities via a Pigovian tax precisely targeted at capital inflows into an economy that is showing signs of a boom. The goal is to reduce the harm of a boom–bust credit cycle.

As Korinek wrote,

> Individual market participants impose externalities in the form of greater financial instability on each other, and the private financing decisions of individuals are distorted towards excessive risk-taking. Prudential capital controls can induce private agents to internalize their externalities and thereby increase macroeconomic stability and enhance welfare.... This presents a textbook policy case:... By imposing Pigouvian taxes or regulations, the decentralized market equilibrium will be efficient. (2011a, Preface, p. 1)

Capital Controls in Practice

Even if there is a perfect textbook case for capital controls, how do they perform outside the textbook in practice? What happens when a policy from the highly stylized world of financial friction theory is imported into the messy real world? So far, the results have been mixed at best. The problem is not just evaluating whether controls on capital inflows lead a country toward a difficult-to-measure efficient market equilibrium. It turns out there is a more basic problem: It is often hard to control capital inflows at all.

Brazil is an actual test case for capital controls: In 2009, Brazil imposed taxes on capital inflows (except for direct investments). Brazil had a comparatively low domestic savings rate of 16% of GDP, so under normal circumstances, capital inflows would be welcomed. However, after the financial crisis, Brazil, like other emerging countries, was experiencing heavy inflows from developed countries with highly accommodative monetary policies. These inflows risked setting off a further appreciation of the already-expensive Brazilian currency, a decline in export competitiveness, and overall financial instability. Brazilian policymakers imposed a tax on foreign purchases of Brazilian equities and fixed-income securities of 2% in 2009, raised the fixed-income tax to 6% in 2010, and eliminated or relaxed most of these controls by 2012.

These capital controls were not successful at the most basic level: They did not control the inflows of capital into Brazil. Forbes, Fratzscher, Kostka, and Straub (2012) found that Brazil's controls had only very short-term (i.e., over periods shorter than three months) effects on inflows and no effect for longer periods. Investors were able to somehow get around the capital controls, thereby defeating their purpose. The controls were "leaky."

Implementation of the Tobin tax presents a parallel test case.[25] Whereas policy experiments to control capital inflows to emerging economies are mostly of interest to government ministers and friction theorists, the concept of a Tobin tax enjoys much wider public support, with many demands that such a tax be imposed.

For instance, Rowan Williams, the former archbishop of Canterbury, called for a Tobin tax on all financial transactions. The Rainforest Action Network is another supporter, as is the organization Friends of the Earth. The 28 member states of the EU authorized 11 countries to proceed with enhanced cooperation on a common system of financial transaction tax (see European Commission 2013). Typically in these efforts, the definition of a "Tobin tax" has migrated from a tax on transactions in a foreign currency designed to give monetary authorities more leeway to a tax on "financial speculators" more generally. What these initiatives ignore is that a Tobin tax has been tried and has failed.

"We tried a Tobin tax and it did not work." This is the conclusion of Magnus Wiberg (2013), an economist formerly at the Swedish Ministry of Finance and Sweden's central bank, the Riksbank. In 1984, Sweden introduced a 0.5% tax rate on the purchase or sale of equities, which rose to 1% in 1986 and was extended to share options. The motivation, according to Wiberg, was to reduce speculation in financial markets and also to increase tax revenues. Interestingly, at that time, Sweden had capital controls on *outflows.*

Despite these controls, the main impact of the transaction tax was to drive capital and trading out of Sweden—to London. According to Wiberg, by 1990, about half of trading in Swedish equities took place in London, whereas trading on Swedish exchanges fell dramatically. The Swedish financial transaction tax is not precisely the same as capital controls, but nonetheless, there are many relevant similarities. The main parallel is the result: Sophisticated investors are able to get around this type of tax. This result was true for Sweden's tax on equity trading as well as for Brazil's taxes on capital inflows.

However, capital controls are not ineffective in all cases. As opposed to the shifting capital controls deployed by Brazil and other emerging economies after the crisis, the nearly permanent capital controls of China have been largely able to stop inflows, according to an empirical analysis by Klein (2012).

Klein drew a distinction between two types of capital controls, which he termed "walls" and "gates." In his terminology, walls (which might also be thought of as deep moats) are near-permanent capital controls that target

---

[25]The Tobin tax, as described earlier, is a small tax on currency transactions. It was first proposed by the Nobel Prize–winning economist James Tobin (1978). In some cases, it can mean a tax on financial transactions in general.

many asset classes. They attempt to isolate, not just insulate, the economy from the vicissitudes of the world's financial system. In contrast, gates are episodic, constantly change their target levels, and include only a small subset of financial assets. Brazil's capital controls fall into the gate category, whereas Chinese controls are walls.

Klein (2012) examined the imposition of capital controls by different countries on different asset classes and found that gates are not effective. They close too slowly or after the fact, with ample room for evasion. He found no evidence that capital controls by South Korea, Brazil, or Chile were able to stop the appreciation of their currencies, a core policy objective of their imposition. Walls, in contrast, are effective. Klein found that during the period of his study (1995–2010), China was largely closed off from the world in terms of financial inflows. He concluded that

> policy discussion on the desirability of capital controls is about episodic controls, because these can be imposed and removed as conditions change. The motivation for imposing episodic controls, however, is often drawn from the experience of countries with longstanding controls. Analyses that do not distinguish between episodic and longstanding controls may not provide accurate guidance for decisions about policy on controls on capital.... These preliminary results raise doubts about assumptions behind recent calls for a greater use of episodic controls. (Klein 2012, p. 317)[26]

Discussion

This new interest, even obsession, of governments and economists with capital controls and causes of international financial crises stems from real-world events. The policy mix in the United States in the years after the 2007 financial shock—namely, the Fed's ultralow interest rates—resulted in large capital flows to emerging market countries that offered higher returns, as shown in **Figure 6**. New theory explains how this so-called hot money effect could be destabilizing. New empirical studies of controls are less conclusive and present

---

[26]An underlying question not directly addressed by this empirical literature is, What was the ultimate purpose of China's closed capital account? Currency intervention could be one answer, with walls playing a critical role. According to this argument, China accumulated US Treasury bonds not because they were a good investment or for precautionary motives but instead to bid up the dollar relative to China's own currency. This effort at currency intervention would have been undermined by capital flows back into China, which could also have resulted in an increase in inflation. Both inflation and currency appreciation were stopped by China's closed capital account. The debate over Chinese mercantilism, including possible currency undervaluation, is highly charged. In any case, the role of capital controls in this debate is very different from that of the policies proposed by new friction models, where capital controls are imposed for macroprudential, rather than mercantilist, reasons. For an analysis of Chinese capital account policies and a model of how they could be used to undervalue the real exchange rate, see Jeanne (2012).

Figure 6. Net Capital Flows to Emerging Markets

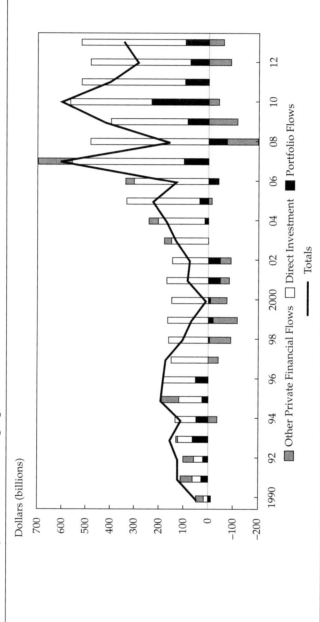

Sources: Forbes (2012, p. 357). Data are from the IMF World Economic Outlook database.

many challenging econometric issues, including problems with endogeneity: Investors may anticipate that controls on inflows are going to be imposed and may, therefore, accelerate inflows in advance of the controls.

For countries worried about spillover effects from the United States, there are many technical issues to consider if capital controls are to be deployed for macroprudential purposes to improve financial stability. First, these concepts are fuzzy and hard to define and measure (see Chapter 4). Policymakers would have to be able to ascertain that the country faced vulnerabilities because it was in the midst of some credit-driven boom–bust cycle that could lead to financial instability. They would have to be able to calibrate the optimal size of the tax on inflows. They would have to distinguish the rationale for the inflows: "hot money" in search of short-term yield versus productive investments in promising projects that could aid the country's long-term growth. Not all capital flows are alike or have equal risks. The highest risks are from short-term debt in a foreign currency. Such debt is vulnerable to Fisher-type debt-deflation loops that end in a fire sale. Hence, when it comes to capital flows, destabilizing flows in short-term debt in a foreign currency are the main subject of concern.

Additionally, unless policymakers are prepared to truly isolate their economy from the financial system, investors are able to get around most capital controls, as seen in Brazil; there is little evidence that short-term capital controls ("gates") are effective at preventing inflows. Given all these implementation challenges, capital controls are, for now, a second-order policy solution.[27]

But the new *theory* of capital controls and of financial frictions in an international context still holds long-term promise for both policymakers and investors. The central insight is that capital inflows tend to be procyclical, with many amplification effects, on the way up but also on the way down. Investors, seeing large inflows into a small country, might now stop to question whether they are participating in a credit-driven boom that can only end badly; that is, they have to be prepared to time these markets. New theory has brought to the forefront of investors' and policymakers' attention risks that may not have previously been fully known or well understood or articulated.

---

[27]A first-order solution might be directly addressing the source of the boom, such as restraining overheated real estate markets by setting strict borrowing limits for mortgages. Another possibility is that a country could set up a sovereign wealth fund as a hedge against the vicissitudes of booms and busts stemming from capital inflows. The fund would grow during the boom period and pay out during the bust. Through such a fund, a country could avoid the implementation challenges associated with capital controls.

The Eurozone Crisis: A Special Case of Capital Flows and Amplifications

> From the scientific point of view, the euro is the most interesting thing. I think it will be a miracle—well a miracle is a little strong. I think it's highly unlikely that it's going to be a great success.... But it's going to be very interesting to see how it works.
>
> —Milton Friedman, *Inside the Economist's Mind: Conversations with Eminent Economists* (edited by Paul A. Samuelson and William A. Barnett)

Background. The economic crisis in the eurozone may seem remote from this discussion of capital flows and financial frictions in an international context. The externalities and amplification effects stemming from inflows are associated with emerging market countries—particularly those that have to borrow in a foreign currency—rather than advanced economies, such as those of the eurozone. Moreover, there is a lack of formal models of how this friction framework might apply to the Economic and Monetary Union, nor is it part of the standard policy discussion of pundits and politicians. Finally, the eurozone crisis has multiple dimensions and drivers beyond credit frictions, many of them fiscal or political. Nonetheless, focusing on capital flows and their destabilizing effects brings fresh insights to the economic crisis of the peripheral eurozone countries and their challenges in becoming competitive with the core countries.

The starting point for any discussion of the eurozone economic crisis is the fact that the eurozone does not meet the criteria for an "optimum currency area" (OCA)—an area characterized by high factor (labor) mobility—as defined by Mundell (1961).[28] Instead, in the eurozone, a heterogeneous group of countries all share a common currency. (Interestingly, Mundell himself was a huge proponent of European monetary unification and is very enthusiastic about the prospects for the euro.)[29]

A survey published by the European Commission titled, possibly mockingly, "The Euro: It Cannot Happen. It's a Bad Idea. It Will Not Last. US Economists on the EMU, 1989–2002" (Jonung and Drea 2009) found that American economists were largely skeptical about the chances for the euro's success—because of their analytical overreliance on optimum currency area theory. The report rejects this framework, noting that OCA theory was "actually

---

[28]An optimal currency area can be larger or smaller than a single country. For instance, Michael A. Kouparitsas of the Federal Reserve Bank of Chicago has argued that the United States does not fit the criteria of an OCA. According to Kouparitsas, the Great Plains, the Southeast, and the Southwest are regions that do not fit and are dissimilar to the rest of the United States (Kouparitsas 2001).

[29]In a *Financial Post* interview with Terence Corcoran (2012), Mundell said, "The euro is a world currency par excellence.... The euro has passed its youth with flying colours."

a North American innovation"; instead, it takes the euro's ongoing existence as self-evident proof of the euro's success and a refutation of this theory. But the crisis in the eurozone transcends OCA theory.

The Setup: Borrowing in a Foreign Currency. The eurozone is a monetary union but not a fiscal union. By definition, all countries entering the currency union give up their monetary independence but governments maintain their fiscal independence. Nonetheless, they issue all debts in euros. They also are subject to exchange rates and interest rates set outside their control. Critically, the euro was set up with only a partially built institutional architecture. In some aspects, it lacked a true central bank. Like other central banks, the European Central Bank (ECB) was concerned with price stability, but it was inconsistent in acting as a lender of last resort for sovereign bond markets. This lack of a liquidity backstop in times of stress for these bonds added to the financial instability of the peripheral governments.[30]

Recall that a key underpinning of the current generation of international friction models, and of earlier models as well, is that the government's borrowing is in a foreign currency. In many ways, this situation describes the countries of the eurozone. Though they are advanced economies with well-developed domestic debt markets, their governments are issuing debt in a currency they do not control—the euro. They are in a position of "original sin," a term that, in economics, refers to a country's inability to borrow abroad in its own currency. These countries are vulnerable to self-fulfilling liquidity crises ending in default.[31]

This overall framework—that eurozone countries essentially are borrowing in a foreign currency—is useful for explaining some of the vulnerabilities the peripheral governments face. But focusing on capital flows adds more detail

---

[30]The ECB does now act as a lender of last resort for sovereign bonds and has stabilized these markets. In this sense, it has broadened its concerns beyond its original narrow focus on price stability to include financial stability as well. For more about this expanded role for the ECB, which is not without controversy, see De Grauwe (2013).

[31]In economics, the term *original sin*, as introduced by Hausmann and Panizza (2003) and Eichengreen, Hausmann, and Panizza (2005), has various meanings but often refers to a government that accumulates debt in a foreign currency because it is unable to borrow in its own currency, which can give rise to financial instability. The original sin literature runs parallel to and in many cases anticipates the later friction literature, which is more concerned with mapping out amplification mechanisms and externalities. See DeRosa (2009) for an excellent explanation of original sin. Corsetti (2010) was the first to observe that the eurozone peripherals, by joining the common currency, have actually entered into a position of original sin. Corsetti's insight has been taken up by De Grauwe and Krugman. For Krugman, the main takeaway from this aspect of the euro crisis story is an argument against austerity—and for fiscal expansionism in the United States. According to Krugman, "Countries that borrow in their own currencies are simply not vulnerable to the kind of self-fulfilling liquidity crises that have afflicted euro debtors" (2013, p. 31).

about the destructive mechanisms involved as well as how the crisis actually unfolded. Unlike competing explanations that focus on OCA theory or the institutional failings of the Economic and Monetary Union, capital inflows and outflows account for the boom–bust pattern observed in the periphery. An increase in wages (driven by capital flows) unaccompanied by an increase in competitiveness is central to this story and to the problems of the eurozone periphery today.

Capital Flows, Competitiveness, and Wages. Free flows of capital are intrinsic to the monetary union (Cyprus's temporary capital controls on outflows are an exception). In a speech in 2013, Vítor Constâncio, vice president of the ECB, described the heady experience of the early days of the euro, the impossibility of capital controls, and the lack of concern about threats caused by inflows:

> I have first-hand experience of the difficulties that periphery countries faced. The European rules on free movement of capital, the objective to create a level playing field for different banking sectors, and the belief in the efficiency of supposed self-equilibrating financial markets, all conspired to make it very difficult to implement any sort of containment policy. Moreover, no one ever predicted that a sudden stop characteristic of emerging economies could occur in the euro area. (Constâncio 2013)

Capital initially flowed into the periphery countries during the early days of the euro to take part in a nascent boom there, in contrast to the low returns offered by the post-reunification German economy.[32] These inflows created a positive feedback loop: Asset prices increased, which led to both an increase in demand and an increase in the value of collateral for further borrowing. The inflows also lowered the real interest rate in peripheral countries. (Recall that under the trilemma, capital inflows are tantamount to a reduction in real interest rates when there is a fixed exchange rate.) Inflation also increased, and the eurozone's one-size-fits-all approach to monetary policy meant that the Taylor rule was violated.[33]

Critically, this ongoing positive feedback loop affected wages, which increased across the eurozone periphery. The high wages were not matched by an increase in productivity or competitiveness. More subtly, the boom also led to an increase in demand for nontradable goods, as opposed to tradable goods;

---

[32]A loophole in banking regulations also played a role in driving flows. Under Basel II regulations, sovereign debt was assigned a risk weight of zero. In a type of carry trade, European banks invested in higher-returning yet allegedly riskless government bonds of the European periphery while borrowing against German government debt (Acharya and Steffen forthcoming).

[33]The Taylor rule holds that when inflation increases, the central bank should raise the nominal interest rate by a higher amount. (One common expression of the Taylor rule is Target interest rate = 1 + 1.5 × Inflation − 1 × Unemployment gap.)

economic growth shifted to housing and services and away from manufactured goods designed for export.[34] The monetary union, designed with the hope of bringing about a convergence of competitiveness, actually caused a divergence. Of course, capital controls were not implemented and could not be implemented by design. Further, these inflows were channeled via banks, which were left highly exposed when the crisis hit.

Amplifications Downwards. Once the crisis hit, the amplification mechanism went into reverse. Real output collapsed and borrowing further decreased, constrained by deteriorating balance sheets and plunging values of collateral and net worth. The peripheral eurozone countries faced a debt-deflation situation similar to that experienced by emerging countries during a crisis: Real interest rates went the wrong direction—up—in real terms, with both price declines and capital outflows contributing to this increase. Nominal wages remained sticky, as **Figure 7** shows. This combination of downward nominal wage rigidity and collapse in demand led to a huge increase in unemployment in the peripheral countries. (Schmitt–Grohé and Uribe 2013).

Several nuances separate this crisis in advanced economics from the negative loop for emerging economies. The latter involves a collapse in the exchange rate, whereas in the case of the eurozone crisis, the nominal exchange rate is fixed, though of course the real exchange rate could still decline. Secondly, capital outflows from emerging markets face balance-of-payments constraints as the local currency is converted to, say, dollars, whereas there is nothing similar to inhibit capital withdrawals from the eurozone periphery.

But in other respects, the peripheral countries closely resembled emerging market economies, with strong capital outflows and Fisher-style debt-deflation loops, culminating in a liquidity crisis and ultimately a sovereign debt crisis. And in the eurozone, there was no lender of last resort.

Discussion. Capital inflows and outflows are merely one component of the eurozone crisis, but their role as a critical driver of the crisis has been largely overlooked. The negative feedback loop between weak sovereigns and weak banks holding their debt was probably more damaging during the darkest days of the crisis. However, capital inflows help explain the increase in wages in the peripheral countries during the boom years and the resulting divergence of

---

[34]Reis (2013) built a model to explore how capital inflows could lead to a misallocation of resources that inhibits productivity growth. Reis's model ties together the literature on credit frictions with a larger literature on total factor productivity and resource misallocation. In Reis's model, capital flows into inefficient firms in the nontradable sector, which find it easier to obtain credit than firms in the tradable sector. One country the model can be applied to is Portugal: Reis argued that the misallocation of resources to slow-growing, consumption-heavy sectors led to the slump in productivity observed in Portugal for much of the 2000s.

Figure 7. Boom–Bust Cycle, Downward Wage Rigidity, and Unemployment in the Eurozone

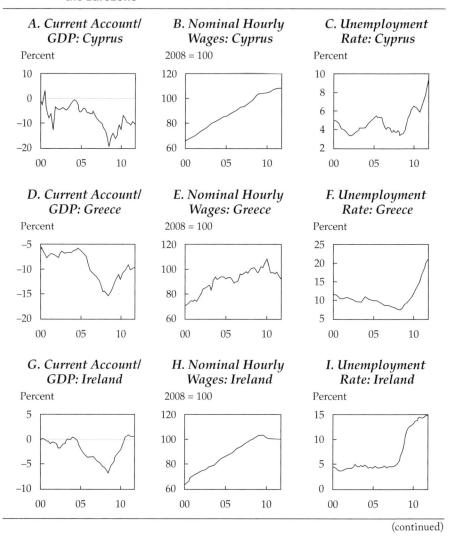

(continued)

competitiveness between the peripheral countries and the core countries (e.g., Germany) that is central to the crisis.[35]

Lowering wages in the peripheral countries to restore competitiveness and employment is a favored policy solution but is not straightforward. The problem

---

[35]Both Lapavitsas (2012) and Sinn (2014) have offered extensive analysis of the competitiveness problems of eurozone peripheral countries and non-peripheral countries (e.g., France) compared with Germany. Though writing from opposite ends of the political spectrum, both economists focused on the role of low wages in German manufacturing as central to this divergence in competitiveness.

Figure 7. Boom–Bust Cycle, Downward Wage Rigidity, and Unemployment in the Eurozone (continued)

J. Current Account/ GDP: Portugal

K. Nominal Hourly Wages: Portugal

L. Unemployment Rate: Portugal

M. Current Account/ GDP: Spain

N. Nominal Hourly Wages: Spain

O. Unemployment Rate: Spain

Sources: Schmitt–Grohé and Uribe (2013). Data are from Eurostat.

goes beyond downward nominal wage stickiness and comes back to original sin. Debts are measured in euros. A decrease in wages or overall internal devaluation might only end up *increasing* liabilities for borrowers, as measured in euros.

Stated differently, effects stemming from an internal devaluation pull in opposite directions for eurozone periphery countries. A decrease in wages might lead to increasing exports and a rise in GDP. But a decline in wages would also make it harder for households to pay off their debts, and if it were accompanied by a price decline, real debt and debt-servicing costs for the country would increase. Hence, a wage cut might actually worsen the real-debt-to-GDP ratio. Overall, the situation is analogous to that facing emerging market governments that have to borrow in a foreign currency: Devaluation has adverse balance sheet effects in that it increases the real debts of households, firms, and governments.

At the moment, it is unclear what the most effective solution is for the eurozone periphery's dilemma. Improved institutions are necessary but not sufficient. Importantly, policy discussions about how to restore competitiveness of the periphery countries through wage cuts usually ignore the impact on real liabilities. The externalities associated with capital flows and their impact on wages and the overall boom–bust cycle are also not discussed. Solutions favored by recent theory—strict capital controls—are, of course, not possible. Nor is easy it to imagine how governments participating in the Economic and Monetary Union can avoid the original sin of issuing debt in a currency they do not control, the euro.

Hence, focusing on capital flow amplification effects and other financial frictions does not reveal immediate solutions for the eurozone crisis. Rather, it reveals unanticipated externalities stemming from participating in a currency union and the complexity of challenges still facing the euro project.

3. Frictions and Asset Pricing

Traditional finance asset pricing models ignore financial frictions. The CAPM, for instance, operates in a frictionless world: Markets are complete, there are no transaction costs, and investors face no leverage constraints.[36] Other asset pricing models, akin to traditional macro models discussed earlier in this book, are composed of only representative agents. They have no explicit role for financial institutions.

Even if most asset pricing models disregard frictions, investors should not: They are the possibly hidden risk that investors are actually being compensated for and one they must consider when building portfolios. Most of these risks, such as the possibility of a liquidity or systemic crisis, are outside of conventional risk measurement practices. The risk taking may be hard to benchmark, but it is occurring nonetheless.

In some ways, even the friction movement in finance has lagged in fully exploring the asset pricing implications of financial frictions. This is surprising because much of the formal methodology for understanding and modeling financial frictions was developed in finance and then imported into macro; finance was ahead of macro (with a few previously discussed exceptions) in terms of developing full-blown models of how a small shock could be amplified by financial institutions and financial markets, leading to persistent aftereffects. The modeling methodologies used by macro and finance pertaining to frictions are very similar—involving negative feedback loops and price externalities— even though the objectives are different. Macro is primarily focused on how these feedback loops affect the real economy and growth. Finance, always more interested in risk and uncertainty, is focused on how a disruption to financial intermediaries impairs liquidity and, ultimately, market efficiency.

In general, contemporary friction modeling is more concerned with financial stability than with asset pricing. The one big exception, explored throughout this chapter, is the "liquidity movement," which is focused on the relationship between liquidity and returns.

Liquidity is a loaded word in finance. It has many different meanings, ranging from market liquidity (ease of trading a security) to funding liquidity (a term with varying definitions but related to investors' or financial intermediaries' ease in obtaining credit with which to buy assets) to available cash balances.

---

[36]Fischer Black (1972) pointed out that investors in the real world face borrowing constraints, though the CAPM assumes otherwise. He used this "friction" to explain why the observed risk–return relationship is much flatter than predicted by the CAPM. His theory about limits to leverage underpins the more recent low-volatility anomaly literature (see Asness, Frazzini, and Pedersen 2012).

Even market liquidity can have slightly different meanings and measures. It can be defined as the speed of a trade, the price impact of a trade, or the bid–ask spread. An entire subfield exists for defining and comparing different measures of market liquidity, with no clear agreement about which measure is "best." Despite the lack of consensus about the precise meaning (and best measure) of liquidity, exploring how this friction affects asset pricing is critically important to investors, particularly after the recent "liquidity crisis."

Background

Behavioral vs. Friction Approaches. In traditional financial theory, markets are frictionless, participants are price takers, and prices should not persist in deviating from fundamentals. These conditions are violated in the presence of frictions. Some frictions identified by finance include the costs to enter a market, the cost of information, and information asymmetries; frictions generated by the financial sector itself are a separate and newer research focus.

The largest research effort to question market efficiency has come from behavioral finance, which has identified multiple anomalies—situations where prices do not reflect fundamental values. Some of the best-known anomalies uncovered by this field include discrepancies in the prices of twin shares (where a single company, such as Royal Dutch and Shell, trades on two separate exchanges with price divergences); the mispricing between 3Com and its subsidiary, Palm; and the price bump following a stock's inclusion in an index (Thaler 2005). Furthermore, there is an entire behavioral economics literature devoted to analysts' forecasts, earnings surprises, and markets' over- or under-reactions to news.

Behavioral economics asserts that these anomalies, broadly speaking, stem from psychology: Irrational noise traders overwhelm markets and rational traders, leading to departures from market efficiency. As Barberis and Thaler (2003) wrote in "A Survey of Behavioral Finance,"

> The traditional finance paradigm seeks to understand financial markets using models in which agents are "rational." Behavioral finance is a new approach to financial markets that has emerged, at least in part, in response to the difficulties faced by the traditional paradigm. In broad terms, it argues that some financial phenomena can be better understood using models in which some agents are not fully rational. (p. 1053)

Moreover, behavioral finance, based on the research program of the psychologists Daniel Kahneman and Amos Tversky, can anticipate the likely behavior of these less than fully rational agents. Kahneman and Tversky have identified numerous heuristics, or mental rules of thumb, that lead to predictable departures from rationality. And one result can be departures from market efficiency.

Financial friction theory is similarly concerned with departures from market efficiency. However, friction theory locates the sources of inefficiency in the various frictions related to financial intermediaries rather than in the psychology of agents or markets. These intermediaries and institutions are themselves largely or even completely missing from behavioral analysis. Friction theory in no way claims that all agents are rational. In fact, friction models could incorporate irrational agents, but this further refinement has yet to be added to most models.[37]

A foundational paper for friction theory in finance is Grossman and Miller (1988). They identified a new agent in financial markets, in addition to buyers and sellers: "market makers"—that is, financial intermediaries. The ability and willingness of market makers to bear risk is critical for the efficiency of markets. A larger concern of friction theory in finance is the relationship between these financial intermediaries and the misfunctioning of financial markets, which occurs in liquidity spirals.

Liquidity Spirals

Liquidity spirals explain how seemingly liquid markets can turn illiquid overnight. Identifying and modeling them has been one of the greatest contributions of friction theory. Formally, these spirals are very similar to the negative amplification loops between financial intermediaries and the real economy discussed in Chapter 1; only here, the loop stays within the financial sector.

The basic intuition behind a liquidity spiral is that a shock to financial intermediaries leaves them financially constrained. As a result, they sell assets, increase margin constraints, or otherwise decrease lending. Each of these moves can set off negative feedback loops that culminate in market liquidity drying up.

Suppose, for example, there is a sudden decline in the price of an asset held by all banks (subprime mortgage-backed securities come to mind). In order to maintain their leverage ratios, banks sell the asset, which creates a price externality: The price of the asset is driven down further. Even healthy banks are affected through mark-to-market accounting. They, too, have to start selling. There are many sellers and no buyers, and markets dry up as a result (Adrian and Shin 2008, 2010, 2011).

In addition to this mark-to-market mechanism, other types of feedback loops can transmit a shock, such as the "margin spiral." During a crisis, margin requirements tighten. Traders delever, and volatility typically spikes as a result. This situation leads to a further tightening of margins, and so on, and market

---

[37]John Cochrane, in his 2011 presidential address to the American Finance Association, criticized behavioral economics and seemed broadly supportive of the friction agenda. He stated, "Arguing over puzzling price patterns is weak. The rational-behavioral debate has been doing this for 40 years rather unproductively. Ideally one should tie price to central items in the models such as the balance sheets of leveraged financial intermediaries" (Cochrane 2011).

liquidity suffers. Other spirals may be operating in tandem with this increase in margins: For instance, speculators may lose money on a trade, forcing them to sell, leading to a further decline in price if many speculators are similarly constrained.

These various spirals can be grouped together into what is known as a liquidity spiral (see **Figure 8**).

Leading models of liquidity spirals—such as those of Brunnermeier and Pedersen (2009) and Gromb and Vayanos (2002)—are not primarily concerned with asset pricing or expected returns. Instead, the real focus is to offer insights into financial fragility and liquidity dry-ups, as well as the negative welfare implications of these feedback loops.

Figure 8.   Liquidity Spirals

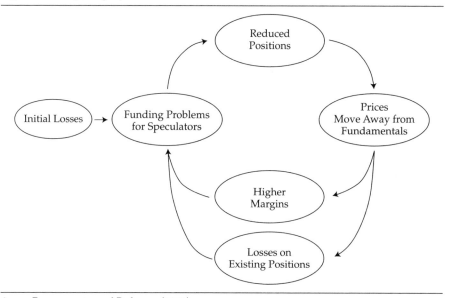

Source: Brunnermeier and Pedersen (2009).

Frictions and Asset Pricing

Market Liquidity. Market liquidity, or lack thereof, affects expected returns in several ways. The literature on this topic is vast (see Adler 2012 for a survey). The goal of this section is to convey the key insights of this research and its empirical methods, as well as some of the limitations and uncertainty associated with it for investors who might want to put these theories into practice.

The core insight of market liquidity and asset pricing is that if markets are less than fully liquid, there is a transaction cost to each trade. The required return on the trade has to increase in some way to compensate investors for this friction. Illiquid assets should offer higher expected returns.

This insight—not part of traditional frictionless asset pricing models, such as the CAPM—has been noted by many theorists. Ibbotson, Diermeier, and Siegel (1984) argued that an asset's "marketability," which includes the concept of liquidity, affects expected return. This very early paper was followed by Amihud and Mendelson (1986) and Amihud, Mendelson, and Pedersen (2013). This literature treats liquidity as a "characteristic" of an asset often measured by the bid–ask spread. Its theoretical conclusions are that (1) this transaction cost should be priced and (2) investors with long time horizons should hold the illiquid asset in order to harvest the higher expected returns of these assets. Although this makes sense in theory and is intuitively compelling, in practice, evidence of a true liquidity premium is mixed. One reason for this lack of evidence is that most asset pricing tests have been performed on highly liquid assets, such as US equities, where such a premium is hard to detect.

A more recent insight is to treat liquidity as a "risk" rather than just as a characteristic of an individual asset. Liquidity affects entire markets and cannot be diversified away. Securities differ in their sensitivity to these marketwide shocks to liquidity. Some assets become highly illiquid during a crisis or experience a plunge in price. Investors should require those assets that are more sensitive to market liquidity shocks to offer higher expected returns to compensate them for the higher risks. That is, there could be a liquidity "factor" or "beta" linking an asset's expected return to the covariance of its price with shocks to market liquidity. Whether there is, in fact, a "liquidity risk" premium is the subject of ongoing debate, discussed later.[38]

These two sets of ideas about how market liquidity—either as a characteristic or as a risk—affects expected returns have been formalized in the liquidity-adjusted CAPM (L-CAPM) of Acharya and Pedersen (2005). This model is the culmination of contemporary theory about market liquidity and asset pricing.

The L-CAPM is similar to the standard CAPM but is augmented to take into account both types of liquidity frictions, as a characteristic and as a risk. Further, Acharya and Pedersen (2005) argued that liquidity as a risk can be subdivided into three distinct "betas," each of which affect expected returns. Investors want to be compensated for the risk of holding assets that become illiquid when the market does—the model's first beta. A second beta, representing the covariance between an asset's return and market liquidity, is negative for typical assets because investors will accept lower returns from assets that hold up well when markets become illiquid. A third beta, representing the covariance of an asset's liquidity with market returns, is also negative for typical

---

[38]The terminology surrounding liquidity is confusing and inconsistent. Readers should be aware that when the literature uses the term "liquidity risk," it more often than not means the risk of illiquidity. Similarly, the "liquidity premium" is actually an "illiquidity premium": higher expected returns for holding illiquid assets.

assets because investors accept lower returns from assets that maintain their liquidity when market returns decline.

Formally, Acharya and Pedersen's (2005) L-CAPM states the following:

$$E_t\left(r_{t+1}^i\right) = r^f + E_t\left(c_{t+1}^i\right) + \lambda_t\left(\beta_t^{r^i,r^M} + \beta_t^{c^i,c^M} - \beta_t^{r^i,c^M} - \beta_t^{c^i,r^M}\right),$$

where

$$\beta_t^{r^i,r^M} = \frac{\text{cov}_t\left(r_{t+1}^i, r_{t+1}^M\right)}{\text{var}_t\left(r_{t+1}^M - c_{t+1}^M\right)} \Bigg\} \ \text{Market beta}$$

$$\beta_t^{c^i,c^M} = \frac{\text{cov}_t\left(c_{t+1}^i, c_{t+1}^M\right)}{\text{var}_t\left(r_{t+1}^M - c_{t+1}^M\right)} \Bigg\} \ \text{Commonality in liqudity}$$

$$\beta_t^{r^i,c^M} = \frac{\text{cov}_t\left(r_{t+1}^i, c_{t+1}^M\right)}{\text{var}_t\left(r_{t+1}^M - c_{t+1}^M\right)} \Bigg\} \ \text{Return sensitivity to aggregate liquidity}$$

$$\beta_t^{c^i,r^M} = \frac{\text{cov}_t\left(c_{t+1}^i, r_{t+1}^M\right)}{\text{var}_t\left(r_{t+1}^M - c_{t+1}^M\right)} \Bigg\} \ \text{Liquidity sensitivity to economic conditions}$$

Required gross returns depend on liquidity as a transaction cost $E(c^i)$, the traditional market beta, and the three liquidity betas described above. βL1 is the covariance of the liquidity of an asset with the liquidity of the market, βL2 is the covariance of a security's return with market liquidity, and βL3 is the covariance of an asset's liquidity with market returns. (In each case, the covariance is scaled, or divided, by the variance of the market return.)

The intuition behind the L-CAPM is straightforward: Assets that are more vulnerable to liquidity shocks should offer higher expected returns given their riskiness. Operationalizing the L-CAPM is far from straightforward, however, because calculating the various betas hinges on calculating the liquidity of the entire market itself. There are several competing measures of liquidity: bid–ask spread, price impact, speed, and price reversals. Different measures lead to different results.

For investors who want to put the L-CAPM into practice, the most tractable price impact measure is Amihud's ILLIQ, which measures the price changes induced by an order flow.[39] The standard academic asset pricing approach is to construct decile portfolios sorted by liquidity risk betas and

---

[39]ILLIQ = Average[|R|/(P × VOL)] = Average(|R|/Dollar volume). ILLIQ measures the daily price response associated with $1.00 of volume. One reason it is so tractable is that it is a low-frequency measure and does not require high-frequency inputs.

then compare the actual returns of the most liquid decile with the least liquid decile for evidence that liquidity is priced.

Using this approach, researchers have shown that liquidity—as a characteristic and a risk—is priced, and for many different asset classes: equities, hedge funds, corporate bonds, even Treasuries (see Adler 2012 for a fuller description). But there are subtleties to the finding that liquidity risk is priced: It can be highly time varying. For instance, there is evidence that liquidity risk in corporate bonds is not priced at all during "normal" periods, only during stress periods (Acharya, Amihud, and Bharath 2010). This may be true for equities as well: Liquidity is priced only during stress periods *following* a liquidity shock; it is not a good warning indicator that a shock is likely to occur.

Other asset pricing tests have not been able to demonstrate that liquidity, as a characteristic or a risk, is indeed really priced at all. Hasbrouck (2006) examined the returns of US equities sorted by liquidity as a characteristic and found only extremely weak evidence that a stock's liquidity is reflected in expected returns.[40]

This inconsistency in results can be explained in part by empirical as well as theoretical limitations to contemporary approaches to market liquidity and asset pricing. Empirically, most asset tests have been performed on highly liquid asset classes, such as US equities, where one would expect any liquidity premium to be small. Data limitations have prevented a comparable body of testing of much more illiquid asset classes, such as timberland. Also, there is little literature specifying quantitative results that investors could use as a benchmark for an expected liquidity premium from an illiquid asset class.

In addition, identifying liquidity as a risk remains technically challenging given the unwieldiness of the L–CAPM, which can produce wildly differing results depending on how liquidity is specified.

A deeper theoretical problem is that the sources of market liquidity shocks are largely "off stage" in the liquidity asset pricing models. Lack of market liquidity can be caused by many different frictions, such as search costs, asymmetric information, imperfect competition where some participants can affect market prices, and financial constraints on financial intermediaries. These differences are fully investigated in the market microstructure literature but

---

[40]There are other inconsistent findings, as well: Acharya and Pedersen (2005) claimed that the L–CAPM shows that illiquid assets also tend to exhibit a high degree of liquidity risk; the two are highly correlated. But Lou and Sadka (2011) found no such relationship. Lou and Sadka's argument is that during a financial crisis, investors are more likely to sell their more liquid, rather than less liquid, stocks to avoid a price impact on markets; hence, these liquid stocks exhibit a higher degree of liquidity risk as measured. This does not, of course, mean that the liquid stocks are really less liquid than the illiquid ones! Furthermore, Sadka (2012) found that for hedge funds, liquidity as a characteristic ("lockup periods") was essentially independent of and not a good proxy for liquidity as a risk.

less so in the asset pricing literature. Even so, different sources of illiquidity can have different impacts on asset prices.[41]

These inconsistencies do not mean that investors should ignore the role liquidity plays in asset pricing; they mean only that investors should acknowledge the limitations of current approaches. That liquidity is priced is only a hypothesis. Nonetheless, on balance, it has ample empirical evidence in its favor. Examples include the finding that restricted stock trades at a steep discount relative to comparable fully liquid equities. Moreover, hedge funds that took high amounts of liquidity risk outperformed funds with lower risk by 6% annually from 1994 to 2008 (Sadka 2012).

Liquidity's impact on expected returns can be seen even in the most liquid asset class of all: US Treasuries. Less liquid, off-the-run Treasuries had an average yield 0.43% higher than their more liquid, on-the-run counterparts over 1961–1980 (Amihud and Mendelson 1986). The final takeaway for investors is that seemingly liquid alternative investments (as measured by liquidity as a characteristic) may still have a lot of liquidity risk (sensitivity to liquidity shocks).

Application: Illiquidity and the Endowment Model

The higher expected returns associated with holding illiquid assets or assets with high liquidity risk might, in fact, be a significant contributor to the "unconventional success" of the endowment model. This model, pioneered by, among others, David Swensen, chief investment officer of the Yale University endowment, involves high allocations to relatively illiquid asset classes, such as private equity or timber. Initially, Swensen (2000) argued that the high potential returns associated with such asset classes was the result of management skills that can be implemented only when there are sufficiently long time horizons, as is true in private equity.

More recently, however, Swensen has explicitly focused on the premium associated with illiquidity itself and attendant risks as critical to these high returns, while still acknowledging that there is a wide dispersion of skill among managers of illiquid assets (Yale Endowment 2010). That is, illiquid investments can generate superior returns compared with liquid assets, but such returns are not guaranteed.

As of 2010, the Yale portfolio was highly illiquid itself, even compared with other endowments, as shown in **Figure 9**.

The endowment's 2010 annual report does not quantify how much of its returns derived from a liquidity premium itself; it argued that "quantitative measures have difficulty incorporating factors such as market liquidity" (Yale Endowment 2010, p. 8).

---

[41]Vayanos and Wang (2012) theoretically derived the conclusion that illiquidity stemming from imperfect competition can reduce expected returns.

Figure 9. Average Endowment and Yale Endowment Liquidity

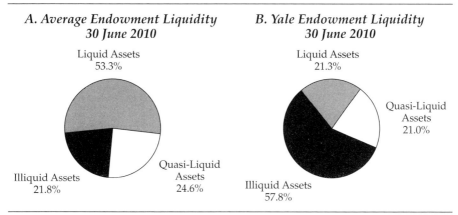

Source: Yale Endowment (2010, p. 18).

Of course, the Yale model has been criticized for being illiquid during the crisis, but that is the very risk being compensated for. Swensen acknowledged that the Yale model was highly illiquid, but he provided the following justification:

> Viewed in the narrow timeframe of the crisis, liquid assets performed better than illiquid assets and safe assets performed better than risky assets. Viewed in a time frame more appropriate for a long-term investor, well-chosen investments in illiquid assets perform better than otherwise comparable liquid assets. (Yale Endowment 2010, p. 3)

In other words, investors with long time horizons can load up on illiquid assets and liquidity risk, as early liquidity theorists argued. But such an approach is far from riskless, as endowments found out. Despite their allegedly infinite time horizons, they had short-term cash flow requirements and faced margin calls. Crises can last for years, and such assumptions need to be built into any cash flow modeling, an exercise apparently not fully undertaken by all endowments. Further, the decline in value of illiquid assets during a crisis means there is a simultaneous decline in their value as collateral for a loan. In many cases, endowments were forced to sell at the worst possible time in deeply illiquid markets.

For individual investors, any attempt at mimicking the endowment model and making a large allocation to illiquid alternatives or alternatives with high liquidity risk must be, therefore, done with extreme care. Even if investors have very long time horizons—which is true when the objective is saving for retirement—their cash flow needs and total portfolio liquidity must be considered. Housing is not particularly liquid. Labor income can be severely affected by a crisis.

Hence, from a total portfolio perspective, the holdings of investors may already be surprisingly illiquid. And some of the biggest risks facing households—loss of a job, the need to sell a house—co-vary strongly with a financial crisis. That is not to say that individual investors must avoid illiquid assets and associated risk premiums altogether; rather, they and their advisers must carefully model their actual liquidity needs before taking on illiquidity risk.

In terms of identifying which assets are actually liquid, liquidity as a characteristic is easy to measure. (Volume is only a very crude proxy, and ILLIQ is a much more precise price impact measure.) Quantifying liquidity risk as a factor is more challenging. Using the L-CAPM to sort assets by liquidity betas variously defined can help investors identify which assets are highly exposed to shocks in market liquidity. Seemingly liquid assets may still have high liquidity risk. For example, Sadka (2012) found that hedge funds touted as highly liquid with no lockups and easy redemptions may, in fact, have high liquidity risk during a crisis.

A straightforward approach to safely holding illiquid assets has been modeled by Siegel (2008), who advocated "liquidity staging"—that is, gradually laddering into illiquid assets, "so that expected future cash flows from these assets partially or fully offset capital calls and other cash requirements." Siegel argued that even with liquidity staging, investors should carefully limit their exposure to illiquid assets so that they do not face cash flow constraints—or, more critically, a requirement to invest new cash—during a crisis.

Funding Liquidity

Funding liquidity, which lacks a consensus definition, refers to the financial constraints facing financial intermediaries. Unlike the market liquidity models described previously, in funding liquidity models, the funding conditions of banks and broker/dealers and their risk-bearing capacity directly affect asset prices.

Though this idea sounds intuitively appealing, it is far removed from traditional asset pricing models that either treat the financial sector like any other economic sector or lack one altogether. For instance, the CAPM has only one factor, the market factor, which does not distinguish between financial firms and other kinds of firms. More complex asset pricing models of more recent vintage actually assume away a financial sector, just as DSGE models do in macro. For example, consumption-based asset pricing models, such as that of Campbell and Cochrane (1999), link asset prices to habit formation and consumption. Consumption is the driver of asset prices; financial institutions are merely a "veil." Hence, once implication of these models, even if not drawn out by Campbell and Cochrane, is that a financial crisis should be no different from any other recession when it comes to asset prices, even though this is not the case.[42]

---

[42]See the discussion in Chapter 1 of Muir's findings comparing the relative impact of recessions, financial crises, and wars.

Moving away from the world of abstract theory, there is robust empirical evidence linking credit supply conditions to asset prices. This evidence sheds light on how financial frictions operate in the real world—sometimes at odds with theory, sometimes confirming it, and sometimes in advance of a full-blown theoretical framework that could explain such results.

There are two sets of ideas regarding how funding liquidity could affect asset pricing, both of which are supported by empirical findings. One is to specify funding liquidity shocks as a new risk factor that explains the cross section of returns; assets exposed to this risk show excess returns. "Funding liquidity risk" is analogous in many ways to "market liquidity risk." That is, securities differ in their sensitivity to funding liquidity shocks. Investors should require those assets that are more sensitive to funding liquidity shocks to offer higher expected returns to compensate them for the higher risks.

A second approach is to examine how credit supply conditions of financial intermediaries (i.e., funding liquidity) directly affect risk premiums and future returns. The looseness or tightness of intermediaries' funding constraints is associated with fluctuations of the risk premiums of markets. Funding liquidity can *predict* expected returns, at least over short time horizons of three months. Risk premiums become compressed as financial intermediaries' funding constraints ease.

A key challenge in trying to pin down the importance of funding liquidity is how to measure it. There are many competing measures of financial intermediaries' funding conditions. There is widespread consensus in the field that funding liquidity can be meaningfully investigated by looking at financial institutions' balance sheets directly. But even here, there are many different balance sheet variables to consider relating to either leverage or net worth.

One active strand of research has been undertaken by researchers at the Federal Reserve Bank of New York: Adrian and Shin (2010); Adrian, Etula, and Shin (2009); Adrian, Moench, and Shin (2013); Adrian, Etula, and Muir (forthcoming). These empirical papers show that broker/dealer leverage is a more important variable for asset pricing than net worth. What is even more striking is that it has predictive power. Leverage can forecast equity and bond returns. Adrian, Moench, and Shin (2013) came to the following conclusion:

> We interpret our finding as a reaffirmation of the importance of credit sup-
> ply conditions for asset pricing. For instance, hedge funds that rely on their
> brokers to construct leveraged positions will care about funding conditions,
> and their returns will depend on the terms of credit offered by their prime
> brokers. (p. 2)

Again, leverage (i.e., funding liquidity) affects expected returns in two ways. Exposure to leverage risk is a priced risk factor that generates positive excess returns. Looking at leverage from a time-series perspective, an increase in broker/dealer leverage is associated with lower risk premiums for a three-month period.

One weakness of using broker/dealer leverage as the key measure of funding liquidity is that shocks to leverage are largely uncorrelated with shocks to market liquidity. In other words, the tight theoretical relationship between funding liquidity and market liquidity, captured in the liquidity spirals of Brunnermeier and Pedersen, does not seem to work in the real world, at least not using this measure of funding liquidity.

However, there are many other competing measures of funding liquidity besides broker/dealer leverage (based on quarterly data). Another type of measure focuses more explicitly on funding conditions and attempts to identify funding liquidity shocks, which is the approach used in the measure developed by J.S. Fontaine of the Bank of Canada.

Whereas the researchers at the Federal Reserve Bank of New York use broker/dealer leverage to measure intermediaries' risk taking—a measure based on quantity—Fontaine uses valuations in the cash and repo markets for US Treasury bonds, a measure based on prices (Fontaine and Garcia 2012; Fontaine, Garcia, and Gungor 2013; work began on the measure by Fontaine and Garcia as early as 2007). The actual factor constructed by Fontaine captures the effects of limits to arbitrage in the cross section of US Treasuries. The intuition behind this approach is that there is a flight to quality—to more liquid Treasuries—when there is a funding liquidity shock.

The flight to quality also affects the ability of arbitrageurs to equalize the yields across nearby Treasury securities because funding conditions tighten in the repo market. The repurchase agreement market is essential to arbitrage price differences between nearby Treasuries.[43] Fontaine's proxy measure is, therefore, informative about funding conditions. We should also expect some connection with broker/dealer leverage because the repo market is the marginal source of funding for broker/dealers.

One advantage of this measure over broker/dealer leverage is that it shows tight correlations between funding liquidity and market liquidity, as predicted by theory (e.g., Brunnermeier and Pedersen 2009).

Chen, Joslin, and Ni (2014) created another measure of funding liquidity, based on deep-out-of-the-money put options bought or sold by financial intermediaries. Fluctuations in the net amount of these options bought or sold are closely tied to financial intermediaries' risk management practices. These fluctuations are informative about intermediaries' funding constraints and their

---

[43]In a personal communication, Fontaine described repos as the principal source of short-term funding for the hedge funds and, to some extent, the investment banks that engage in Treasury bond arbitrage. Thus, a healthy repo market is essential for keeping Treasury bond prices in line with one another.

effective risk aversion. Chen et al. (2014) found that their measure is predictive of excess returns over a subsequent three-month period.

These different measures of funding liquidity are not tightly correlated with each other. For instance, Fontaine's measure is significantly correlated with the Treasury–Eurodollar (TED) spread and the VIX, an equity volatility index; this is not the case for the measure of Chen et al. (2014), which has only a 0.33 correlation with the TED spread in their time series.

So far, there has been no statistical "horse race" fully comparing these measures with each other or with actual broker/dealer leverage. The actual broker/dealer balance sheet information is available only on a delayed quarterly basis via Fed flow of funds data.

Therefore, these measures, or at least some of them, by definition must be noisy. The real underlying challenge is that theory in this area is sparse. It is not clear what really drives these changes in funding liquidity. It is not clear why these changes affect asset prices; all that is clear is that the research that has been discussed all shows some sort of empirical relationship.

The disagreements about how best to measure funding liquidity, both in theory and in practice, are not the signs of a field in disarray. Instead, they are evidence that this area of asset pricing is not yet in a "classical situation" of finality, repose, and lack of curiosity about new answers, as discussed in the Prologue of this book. The field is at an earlier, more active stage of development and research, as well as struggle. Perhaps someday there will be a widely agreed-on, non-noisy measure of funding liquidity, but there are many challenges.

Researchers who are trying to identify such a predictive measure are engaged in a task worthy of Sisyphus: Once a measure becomes widely known and is shown to have true predictive power, it will quickly become arbitraged away or intermediaries will change their behavior. The research struggle is still interesting and important. The unfolding story around financial intermediaries' funding constraints and rise and fall in leverage offers insights into their changing "risk appetite," which might, in turn, be driving markets' risk premiums. The right measure of funding liquidity could someday predict the "risk-on" (short-term bullish) and "risk-off" (short-term bearish) tendencies that markets today often display.

4. Macroprudential Policies and Systemic Risk

> Risk premia and volatilities [are] unusually low precisely when risk is highest. What looks like low risk is, in fact, a sign of aggressive risk-taking.
>
> —Claudio Borio, "Rediscovering the Macroeconomic Roots of Financial Stability Policy: Journey, Challenges, and a Way Forward"

Of all the topics discussed in this book, the interrelated concepts of systemic risk and macroprudential policies are theoretically the least developed. Where theory exists at all, current empirical work is in even worse shape; there is little consensus on how to measure systemic risk, with many measures being unreliable and subject to challenge. Despite these problems, finding ways to measure systemic risk and implementing macroprudential policies to curtail it are some of the most pressing issues of the post-crisis era. Regulators and policymakers are rightfully determined to prevent another systemic crisis.

This chapter starts with some of the theory behind macroprudential policies and systemic risk, before moving on to describe current empirical measures of systemic risk and related regulatory efforts. Chapter 5 discusses some of the challenges of implementing macroprudential polices as well as the role of monetary policy in curbing systemic risk. The main objective of the current chapter is to convey that there are two dimensions to systemic risk: risks that are building up over time, consisting of a surge in credit, and risks of contagion or spillovers at a particular point in time if a large or interconnected financial institution were to fail. Each type of risk calls for a specific macroprudential policy response.

Definitions

What is meant by *macroprudential policies* and *systemic risk*? The terms are slippery: Each has many different definitions and interpretations—all of which can be used to promote widely varying policies. It is fair to say that the concepts are best defined in opposition to each other: Macroprudential policies are ones designed to reduce systemic risk.

Moreover, macroprudential policies can also be defined in contrast to traditional "microprudential policies." These policies focus on individual institutions, whereas macroprudential policies focus on the stability of the entire financial system as a whole. The intuition behind this distinction is that what is prudent for an individual financial institution (microprudential) is no guarantee of stability for the overall financial system. For instance, during the 2007–09 crisis, individual banks made adjustments to their balance sheets, including deleveraging and increasing margins, that were prudent for each bank when considered in isolation and were consistent with regulation targeting individual institutions. However, these actions created spillover effects for other banks, eventually leading to liquidity spirals and frozen markets.

A formal and precise definition of the term *macroprudential* has been put forward by the Bank for International Settlements (Clement 2010): "The term refers to the use of prudential tools with the explicit objective of promoting the stability of the financial system as a whole, not necessarily of the individual institutions within it" (p. 65). A BIS-devised definition of macroprudential is important because of the institution's stature as a sort of central bank for central banks but also because of the BIS's historical role in originating the term *macroprudential* itself: The word appears to have been coined at a 1979 BIS meeting about risks in international lending that could threaten the global financial system.[44]

The word *macroprudential*, once esoteric, is now in common use, at least among central bankers, regulators, editorial writers, and those concerned with post-crisis regulatory policies. Although it is a buzzword, the term is not straightforward and there is no universal agreement on what macroprudential policies actually consist of. There is still a certain circularity to the concept because even if there is an unspoken consensus that macroprudential policies are ones designed to promote financial stability, "there is no commonly shared definition of financial stability" (Financial Stability Board 2012, p. 13).

Macroprudential: Theoretical Underpinnings

Though the definition of *macroprudential* remains vague and identification of effective policy instruments is even more up for grabs, the conceptual underpinning of this term and related policies is clear, at least at a theoretical level.

Macroprudential policies grapple with departures from the frictionless, idealized Arrow–Debreu world. Regardless of the specific policy instrument used, the economic foundation and justification for these policies is rooted in the need to correct market imperfections.

There are several large categories of market imperfection that justify macroprudential regulation. The first concerns externalities related to financial

---

[44]At this 1979 meeting, according to an internal history of the BIS (Clement 2010), committee chairman W.G. Cooke of the Bank of England voiced concern that microprudential problems could affect the wider economy and, hence, become "macroprudential" in nature. Also in 1979, a definition of this term close to contemporary use, and one with a focus on regulation and supervision, appeared in another BIS research report, "The Use of Prudential Measures in the International Banking Markets." The report argued that "the macroprudential approach considers problems that bear on the market as a whole as distinct from an individual bank and which may not be obvious on a microprudential level" (as quoted by Clement 2010, p. 61). These documents were for internal use only; the first public appearance of the term *macroprudential* in a BIS publication was in 1986, and in this publication, the word was used in the context of policies that promote broader financial stability (Clement 2010).

frictions and the damage financial intermediaries can impose on each other and the real economy.

The failure of a single "too-big-to-fail" bank is a very clear example of an externality: It causes huge collateral damage to the financial system. The impact of capital flows on emerging economies is another example of an externality—hence, the argument about the need for controls on capital inflows, for macroprudential reasons.

In general, these types of externalities are known as *pecuniary* externalities, meaning they involve price spillovers in the financial system, leading to volatility, instability, and, ultimately, inefficiency. The purpose of macroprudential regulation is to internalize these externalities—that is, to incentivize institutions to act in the interest of financial system stability and not just in their own interests. The bulk of this book—as well as current policy discussions—is focused on these kinds of externalities related to the financial system. The recent financial crisis made these financial frictions—that is, departures from idealized financial markets—particularly salient.

However, there is a second broad type of market imperfection: This one takes place in the real economy rather than in the financial system. The real (nonfinancial sector) economy can set off its own macro demand shocks and, hence, is a potential source of systemic risk. After all, the initial "shock" that set off the financial crisis in the United States arose in subprime mortgages. Households and firms can become dangerously leveraged and face their own risk of fire sales and painful deleveraging. Macroprudential policies could include those that mitigate this risk of deleveraging by households by setting strict debt limits for households in the first place, in contrast to current US mortgage and student loan policies. In general, most macroprudential policies, after the financial crisis, have remained narrowly focused on banking regulation rather than on systemic risks that could arise from households or corporations (Jeanne and Korinek 2014).

A third broad type of market imperfection concerns bailout risk and the moral hazard that can occur because of government guarantees. Sometimes bailout risk is called "risk shifting"—shifting risk to the government and, eventually, the taxpayer. Typically, bailout risk is a concern of microprudential regulation, but if it becomes system-wide, it could be classified as macroprudential (which again shows that these classifications remain imprecise). For instance, all banks may load up on the same risk, in a "herd." If they all have the same risk exposure, the government will likely be forced to bail them out collectively even if no single bank involved is too big to fail. Such herding has been called "too many to fail" and is an example of the distortions caused by the likelihood, or perceived likelihood, of a bailout.[45]

---

[45]For a typology of different "paradigms" of macroprudential policies, see de la Torre and Ize (2009).

All three types of market imperfections can, in a general sense, be termed *systemic risks* because they threaten the stability of the financial system. All call for the policy responses classified as macroprudential. But before specific policy tools can be implemented, these imperfections need to be identified—and measured—given the cliché that it is hard to manage what you cannot measure. A focus on measurement, therefore, has become critically important from a policy perspective. Enter systemic risk measures.

Systemic Risk

Background. The definition of systemic risk—and finding ways to measure it—is as problematic as, or even more so than, the definition of macroprudential policies. There are hundreds of definitions and measures of systemic risk. There is no consensus on which definition regulators should use, nor is there a consensus on which indicator is most important in predicting a crisis, nor are the theoretical underpinnings for the concept of systemic risk clear.

Currently, systemic risk "does not yet have a rigorous singular definition" (Moore and Zhou 2014, p. 2), but in general, it is concerned with threats to the stability of the financial system. It is focused on surges in credit as well as the externalities that the failure of a large or interconnected financial institution poses to the other banks and the real economy, through contagion effects and feedback loops. Macroprudential regulation is designed to correct these externalities.

Some academics are skeptical about current efforts to measure systemic risk, pointing to the paucity of theory to support these measures. For instance, the economist Lars Peter Hansen (2013) has argued that there are challenges to measuring systemic risk from both a theoretical and an empirical perspective. Given the lack of formalization of the concept of systemic risk, he claimed that it is naive to try to identify a simple quantitative measure before more rigorous theoretical models are developed and evaluated. Hansen's concern is that measurement is proceeding well in advance of theory because of regulatory pressure, which "requires shortcuts and can proliferate superficial answers" (2013, p. 1).

There is indisputably a proliferation of systemic risk measures. A survey of systemic risk analytics by the Office of Financial Research (OFR) of the US Treasury identified 31 different ways to measure systemic risk (OFR 2012).

The Bank of England's Financial Policy Committee, which is responsible for monitoring and taking action to reduce systemic risk, relies on 17 systemic risk indicators. A draft policy statement from the Bank of England (BOE), setting out some of these measures, acknowledged that "no single set of indicators can ever provide a perfect guide to systemic risks, or to the appropriate policy responses."

There is a reason for this proliferation of measures of systemic risk in advance of theory: Regulators are not waiting for academic levels of precision and theoretical perfection to proceed. Systemic risk is already embedded in legislation, with specific measures informing the judgment of policymakers.

For instance, under Basel III, the guidance for national authorities setting a countercyclical buffer states, "Each jurisdiction will be required to monitor credit growth and make assessments of whether such growth is excessive and is leading to the buildup of systemwide risks" (BIS 2010, p. 2). Similarly, in the United Kingdom, the statutory responsibility of the BOE's Financial Policy Committee is "identifying, monitoring and taking action to remove or reduce systemic risks."[46]

In other words, the discussion about systemic risk is not merely academic: There are mandates to measure systemic risk and take action now.

Two Types of Systemic Risk. Systemic risk has two distinct dimensions: (1) risks that build up over time and (2) the contagion and spillover risks posed by the failure of interconnected institutions at a particular point in time. The buildup over time of systemic risks generally involves surges in credit. This buildup in credit is an early warning indicator for banking crises. The second category of systemic risk is the interconnectedness of financial institutions and the risk of contagion that could result from a bank's or market's failure. It requires a different set of risk measures and macroprudential responses.

In **Figure 10**, the cube illustrates the different forms of systemic risk, their origins, and where they overlap.

Traditionally, macroeconomists focused on the time dimension of broad macroeconomic risks that were building up in the system and thereby increasing the likelihood of a financial crisis. Financial economists primarily focused on the point-in-time dimension and on identifying systemically important institutions or the common exposures of institutions. After the financial crisis, both macro and financial economists have come to acknowledge that the two dimensions of systemic risk are important, and both use this broader framework.[47]

Systematic risk, a concept that practitioners may already be familiar with, is distinct from systemic risk. The clearest description of these differences is

---

[46]Bank of England (www.bankofengland.co.uk/financialstability/pages/fpc/default.aspx).

[47]Philipp Hartmann, head of the Financial Research Division of the ECB, has argued that there is, in fact, an additional form of systemic risk: the financial system's vulnerability to an extreme external macro shock. (Hartmann created the ECB's systemic risk cube, shown in Figure 10, which depicts this macro shock type of systemic risk. He was the first economist to distinguish between the different types of systemic risk.) Hartmann has argued that the recent global financial crisis was the result of an endogenous credit boom and bust and, hence, is better captured by the analytical framework of risks building up over time rather than that of an external shock. In contrast, the crisis in the Finnish banking system triggered by the fall of the Soviet Union is an example of a systemic crisis caused by an external macro shock. Macro stress tests are the primary tool that policymakers can use to assess how a hypothetical external macro shock would affect a country's banking system (ECB 2010).

Figure 10. The Systemic Risk Cube

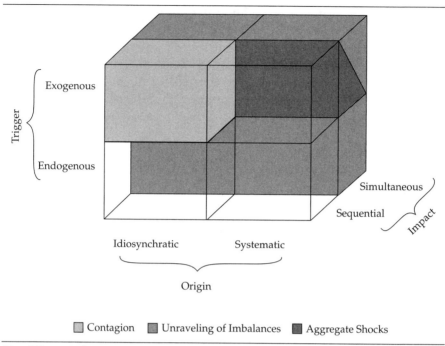

Notes: "Contagion" represents cross-sectional risks at a particular point in time, such as the failure of a too-big-to-fail bank. "Unraveling of imbalances" refers to the collapse of the financial cycle and of risks that have been building up over time.
Source: ECB (2010, p. 139).

offered by Kritzman (2012): Systematic risk is the risk to a company caused by its exposure to the market; systemic risk is the risk to the market caused by its exposure to a company.[48]

■ *Risks building up over time: Measurement and macroprudential response.* Systemic risk measures that include a time dimension focus on excessive credit growth. The intuition behind this approach is that credit booms can lead to subsequent busts, an idea that comes straight from Minsky. The specific systemic risk measure informing most policymaking in this area is the credit-to-GDP gap. This measure captures deviations in the credit-to-GDP ratio over time (the "gap" between the current ratio and some measure of the normal or healthy ratio).

The inputs used are broad and include bank credit and consumer credit. Unlike the gap measure, simple bank-based leverage ratios miss out on the importance of household credit.

---

[48]Paraphrased by the author from a presentation by Mark P. Kritzman (2012). The related paper is Kinlaw, Kritzman, and Turkington (2012).

©2014 The CFA Institute Research Foundation

The credit-to-GDP gap, and the buildup in credit it is trying to measure, is essentially synonymous with the financial cycle, described in Chapter 1. Again, the credit cycle is about 16 years long, on average, in contrast to the much higher-frequency business cycle. According to Borio (2012), "Peaks in the financial cycle are associated with banking crises" (p. 4).

Economists have had trouble modeling the endogenous booms and busts that characterize the financial cycle, so risk metrics in this area are not supported by well-developed formal theory. Most formal macro friction models instead model the feedback loops once a crash occurs, with the crash being driven by an external shock. This lack of modeling means that economists have little theory to explain why a surge in credit should automatically lead to a crisis; they mainly have only "Minskian" intuition that a credit boom sows the seeds of a bust. Furthermore, the credit-to-GDP gap in no way gives a precise indication of when the bust might occur; it does not predict actual turning points, only growing "imbalances" in credit. Overall, macroprudential policy lacks a Taylor-like rule for how to respond to the financial cycle as measured by credit-to-GDP gap.

Even if it is not clear why the credit-to-GDP gap works, it is clear that it does work: It has been shown, empirically, to be a very good indicator of looming financial distress. It is also unusual in the sense of being an early warning indicator of a potential banking crisis; in contrast, systemic risk measures that identify too-big-to-fail banks are contemporaneous, rather than leading, indicators. Given these unusual empirical qualities, the credit-to-GDP gap is enshrined in the Basel III framework as a guide for the setting of countercyclical capital requirements for banks.

There are many technical problems associated with calculating the credit-to-GDP gap. Perhaps this is why it is used only as a guide under Basel III, rather than as a mechanical rule. For one, it is not a particularly reliable real-time measure. It is very slow in signaling that a crisis has actually arrived. Moreover, its calculation depends on estimates of macro data, and these are subject to frequent revision. Edge and Meisenzahl (2011), economists at the Fed, found that the unreliability in estimates necessary for calculating the credit-to-GDP gap meant that the measure provides a poor foundation for policymaking. However, given that the credit-to-GDP gap is still the preeminent time-dimension measure of systemic risk and that it informs bank regulation, it is likely the measure will be improved on rather than discarded altogether.

One way to improve it was proposed by Bush, Guimaraes, and Stremmel (2013), who advocated adding price-of-risk indicators or proxies for them, such as market volatility, to augment the bank balance sheet quantities currently in the measure. Price-of-risk measures, such as spreads, are much faster moving than balance sheet variables and have different cyclical properties, which can help with identifying the phase of the cycle in real time. Adding measures of this kind in some formalized way to the credit-to-GDP gap can be useful for policymakers trying to decipher what phase of the financial cycle they are in and what countercyclical actions to take.

The main macroprudential policy tool used to address the growing surge in credit is countercyclical capital buffers. These buffers force banks to build up additional capital that can be released in a downturn. According to Drehmann and Tsatsaronis (2014), the main point of the buffer is to "protect banks from the effects of the financial cycle" (p. 1).[49]

■ *Contagion and spillover risk: Measurement and macroprudential response.* The financial system can also become unstable because of spillovers or contagion caused by the failure of a too-big-to-fail bank or smaller banks that are highly interconnected. Risk measures in this area attempt to capture the common exposures and financial interdependence that characterize this risk and the financial fragility that can result.

Contagion-type risk measures are essentially contemporaneous, identifying where the interlinkages are right now. They are different from measures that provide a warning of a crisis to come, such as the gap measure that tracks the buildup of credit. Contagion-type measures are adept at identifying institutions that are systemically important because they are either too big or too interconnected to fail. They are also concerned with mapping out financial networks, common exposures, and correlations and with tracking how a bank failure would cause spillover effects to the rest of the financial system.

Contagion and spillover risks can be assessed by using two different types of tool. One type consists of counterfactual simulation of interbank contagion. In this exercise, the analyst assumes one bank fails and explores the impact on other financial institutions.

A second type of tool uses market indicators, such as equity prices or bond prices, and then explores the market impact and spillover caused by an extreme decline in market prices. There are many, many measures in this area.

One leading measure is CoVaR, developed by Adrian and Brunnermeier (2011), which measures the VaR of the whole financial sector conditional upon an individual institution being in distress. (The "Co" in CoVaR is short for "conditional, contagion, or contributing"—all words that emphasize the systemic nature of the measure.) CoVaR can be used to estimate which institutions contribute most to systemic risk as well as which are most exposed in times of financial distress.

Duffie (2011) proposed a new measure, "10 by 10 by 10," which uses a network-based approach and a new reporting requirement to analyze risk exposures of financial institutions. It relies on both counterfactual simulation

---

[49]For the exact Basel III rules about setting the buffer, see BIS (2010).

and market-based indicators: Regulators would evaluate 10 different stress scenarios and the resulting losses suffered by financial institutions. The advantage of Duffie's (2011) approach is that "the joint exposure of the system to particular stress tests and particular entities (or chains of entities) could as a result be clarified."

The Basel Committee on Banking Supervision identifies globally important banks through a variety of indicators that "reflect the size of banks, their interconnectedness, the lack of readily available substitutes for the services they provide, their global (cross-jurisdictional) activity and their complexity" (Galati and Moessner 2011, p. 4). A bank may be unique in providing custodial services, and its failure would be very damaging to the financial system; the Basel-type measure would pick up the systemic importance of such an institution, even if it were not apparent from raw data or other cross-sectional risk measures.

There is a huge variety of macroprudential policy tools under consideration that can be used to address the contagion, spillover, and other systemic risks posed by systemically important financial institutions. For instance, these institutions could be supervised more intensely, be forced to undergo stress tests, provide living wills, face heightened liquidity requirements, or even be broken up. The Volcker rule, which prohibits (commercial) US banks from engaging in proprietary trading or sponsoring a hedge fund or private equity fund, is an example of a structural reform that can reduce the risks posed by these institutions. The Dodd–Frank Act has a number of provisions in this area, but they require implementation. Also, Dodd–Frank has several loopholes.[50]

One macroprudential tool that directly targets contagion risks is capital surcharges on systemically important institutions. These surcharges create a capital buffer that offers protection in case of a failure. If these institutions are viewed by the market as too big to fail, they receive a huge implicit subsidy of lower funding costs because the market believes the government will bail them out.[51] A capital surcharge, if calibrated correctly, could wipe out this unfair advantage that too-big-to-fail institutions have over other financial companies.

The G–20 is broadly supportive of the idea of capital surcharges on systemically important financial institutions, but these surcharges have not been implemented in the United States.[52]

---

[50]For more about the Dodd–Frank Act, see the subsequent section, "CFA Institute and Systemic Risk."

[51]Andrew Haldane of the Bank of England claimed that "over the period 2002 to 2007, the implied annual subsidy to the world's largest banks averaged $70 billion per year using a ratings-based measure. That is roughly 50% of the average post-tax profits of these banks over the period" (Haldane 2012, p. 4).

[52]Both the ECB and the BIS have provided technical details on how the surcharge could be calculated and its policy objectives. See ECB (2010, p. 151) and "Global Systemically Important Banks: Assessment Methodology and the Additional Loss Absorbency Requirement" (BIS 2011).

What all these macroprudential tools—those designed to address the buildup of credit and those that address contagion—have in common is that they are designed to improve the *resilience* of the financial system. They are not designed to completely curb the financial cycle or end the possibility of contagion altogether.

But it is still unclear whether macroprudential policies, even if accurately calibrated and fully implemented, can effectively mitigate systemic risks. These tools might not be enough to truly ensure the resilience of the financial system. Other solutions might be needed, such as the use of monetary policy. This issue is discussed further in Chapter 5.

CFA Institute and Systemic Risk

CFA Institute has two separate initiatives related to systemic risk.[53]

SFMI and Systemic Risk

CFA Institute's Standards and Financial Market Integrity (SFMI), which focuses on advocacy, is working toward a common definition of systemic risk. The definition and conceptual framework will be used in CFA Institute's continuing education efforts. The following is an excerpt of the definition being proposed, which is still a work in progress:

> Systemic risk is the risk of a large-scale failure of a financial system whereby a financial crisis is realized when providers of capital (depositors, investors, capital markets) lose trust in either the users of capital (banks, borrowers, leveraged investors, etc.) or in a given medium of exchange (e.g., US dollars, Japanese yen, gold, silver, etc.). In losing trust, the providers of capital tighten standards, expand covenants, cease new loans, and/or recall funds (call-in loans, withdraw deposits, etc.) or sell currencies they perceive to be at risk. Whatever reason the providers of capital lose trust, once they limit or withdraw capital, the crisis then cascades from unhealthy institutions to the otherwise healthy institutions, which is a defining feature of systemic risk.[54]

The proposed definition has been developed by Ron Rimkus, content director, economics and alternative investments, CFA Institute. It reflects his larger framework for understanding systemic risk, which has loss of trust

---

[53]Although the CFA Institute Research Foundation, the publisher of this book, is an independent 501(c)(3) organization with governance and operations separate from those of CFA Institute, the foundation's activities "support the CFA Institute mission of promoting the highest standards of ethics, education, and professional excellence for the ultimate benefit of society" (see www.cfainstitute.org/learning/foundation/pages/index.aspx).

[54]This quote is from a 2014 e-mail from Ron Rimkus to the author.

at its core. Leverage, interdependence, and the inability to absorb losses are transmission mechanisms.

This definition and framework are currently in working-paper form. SFMI is in the process of coalescing this working paper into a finalized definition that will be used in continuing education and discussions with regulators.

The Systemic Risk Council

The Systemic Risk Council (SRC) is an independent project jointly created by CFA Institute and the Pew Charitable Trusts. It

> is a private sector, nonpartisan body of former government officials and financial and legal experts committed to addressing regulatory and structural issues relating to systemic risk in the United States. It has been formed to provide a strong, independent voice for reforms that are necessary to protect the public from financial instability.[55]

The SRC meets regularly and files comment letters. Its advocacy efforts focus primarily on identifying "structural" weaknesses that can cause or contribute to systemic risk. Its advocacy addresses several important topics, discussed next.

Money Market Funds. The SRC has issued comments arguing that money market funds should move to floating net asset value, which already applies to all other mutual funds.

Too Big to Fail. Though the Dodd–Frank Act makes a number of changes to help address concerns about institutions perceived as too big to fail (TBTF), many provisions require implementing regulations. The SRC has urged action regarding TBTF on several fronts. It wants to make sure that potentially systemic, large, complex financial institutions have sufficient capital to reduce the probability of failure and that the regulatory capital rules are simplified. Traditional risk-based capital requirements rely heavily on recent events and on internal risk modeling. The SRC has advocated reducing reliance on internal risk models for setting regulatory capital levels and applying a parallel, simple leverage requirement to buttress weaknesses in these risk-based capital frameworks.

In terms of potentially systemically important nonbank financial institutions, the SRC argues in favor of designating such firms for heightened supervision by the Federal Reserve and applying Dodd–Frank "living will" provisions that require firms to credibly show they can fail in traditional bankruptcy without destabilizing the financial system.

---

[55]CFA Institute (www.cfainstitute.org/learning/products/publications/contributed/Pages/systemic_risk_council_-_a_call_to_action.aspx).

Overall, these positions seek to address both the substantive and the market perception problems related to TBTF. To truly end TBTF, a firm must be able to fail without destabilizing the system and the market must understand and believe that the firm can fail. To hold regulators and institutions accountable for progress on substance and to address market perceptions, the SRC is in favor of increased transparency, including more information about living wills.

Self-Funding of the SEC and the Commodity Futures Trading Commission. The SRC has argued that the SEC and the Commodity Futures Trading Commission should be funded the same way other regulatory agencies are—that is, self-funded. Not only do these agencies have enormous responsibilities (particularly after Dodd–Frank), but they also must rely on unpredictable funding from Congress.

Central Clearinghouses. Dodd–Frank requires that standardized swaps be subject to mandatory clearing at regulated clearinghouses. Clearing can improve transparency and reduce counterparty credit, but clearinghouses themselves can pose systemic risks. Though Dodd–Frank added additional oversight for potentially systemically important clearinghouses (and other so-called designated financial market utilities), this regime is "weaker" than the enhanced prudential regime outlined earlier and, at the same time, provides these firms with potential access to the Federal Reserve. This structure can create perverse incentives that encourage size and riskiness among these firms. The SRC advocates more robust risk management and transparency requirements for central clearinghouses, as well as living will/resolution planning in the case of their failure.

Making Regulators Work Better Together. This final area of advocacy concerns improving the nature of regulation itself. Regulators often work in silos, which was true before the crisis but is still true today. In particular, the SRC argues that there is a need for a strong Financial Stability Oversight Council and an improved Office of Financial Research to provide timely information that is freely shared with all regulators and the public.

Ricardo Delfin, executive director to the chairman and special adviser at the SRC, says,

> While the structure of the US financial system is in a much better position than it was before the crisis, a number of key structural weaknesses remain. We must implement strong, simple reforms now so that our markets can function fairly and freely in good times and in bad. Taxpayers and policymakers should never again be asked to choose between bailouts or financial collapse.[56]

---

[56]This official comment from Delfin is from correspondence with the author.

5. A Look Back and a Look Ahead: Financial Frictions, the Financial Crisis, and the Path to Reform

The 2007–09 Crisis

> Financial crises are everywhere and always due to problems of short-term debt.
>
> —Douglas Diamond, "Lessons from the Credit Crisis"

Financial crises are all alike, as Diamond (2009) noted, related to banks' core activity of maturity transformation and reliance on short-term funding to make long-term loans. But in other key respects, every crisis is different. For instance, what is the epicenter? How does the crisis propagate? How is it eventually resolved? In this chapter, I will take a look back at the 2007–09 financial crisis and a look ahead at the continuing attempts at reform. The chapter will convey larger lessons learned—in terms of improved economic policies to ensure greater financial stability—as well as how the social science of economics itself could be improved on in some of its practices, which includes a greater emphasis on financial frictions. These are vast and still-unfolding topics. I will examine them through a very narrow prism of several defining financial frictions and will describe new insights that can be gleaned from this emphasis.

The 2007–09 crisis in the United States was certainly a crisis of short-term debt, with a liquidity mismatch between financial intermediaries' long-term illiquid investments and short-term liabilities. What was novel is where the financial crisis occurred: in the US "shadow banking" system.

The term *shadow banking* itself only dates to 2007. It was coined by PIMCO economist Paul McCulley, who defined the system as consisting of highly leveraged intermediaries who "fund themselves with uninsured short-term funding" (McCulley 2009, p. 1). Such intermediaries include hedge funds and, according to Ben Bernanke, "securitization vehicles, asset-backed commercial paper (ABCP) conduits, money market mutual funds, markets for repurchase agreements (repos), investment banks, and mortgage companies" (2012, p. 4).

These financial institutions engage in bank-like activities, primarily securitization, but without access to publicly provided sources of liquidity (the Fed) or insurance (the Federal Deposit Insurance Corporation, or FDIC). The lack of a guaranteed government liquidity backstop creates unusual vulnerabilities, including the possibility of runs, which were long thought to have been eliminated from modern banking systems.

Though the term *shadow banking* implies there is something "shadowy" about these institutions, shadow banking is, in fact, the primary form that financial intermediation has taken today (Mehrling, Pozsar, Sweeney, and Neilson 2012). This system may have been operating in the shadows, but before the crisis, at least, it was larger than the traditional banking system. It had $22 trillion in liabilities as of June 2007, compared with traditional banking liabilities of $14 trillion (see **Figure 11**).[57]

Figure 11.   The Rise of Shadow Banking

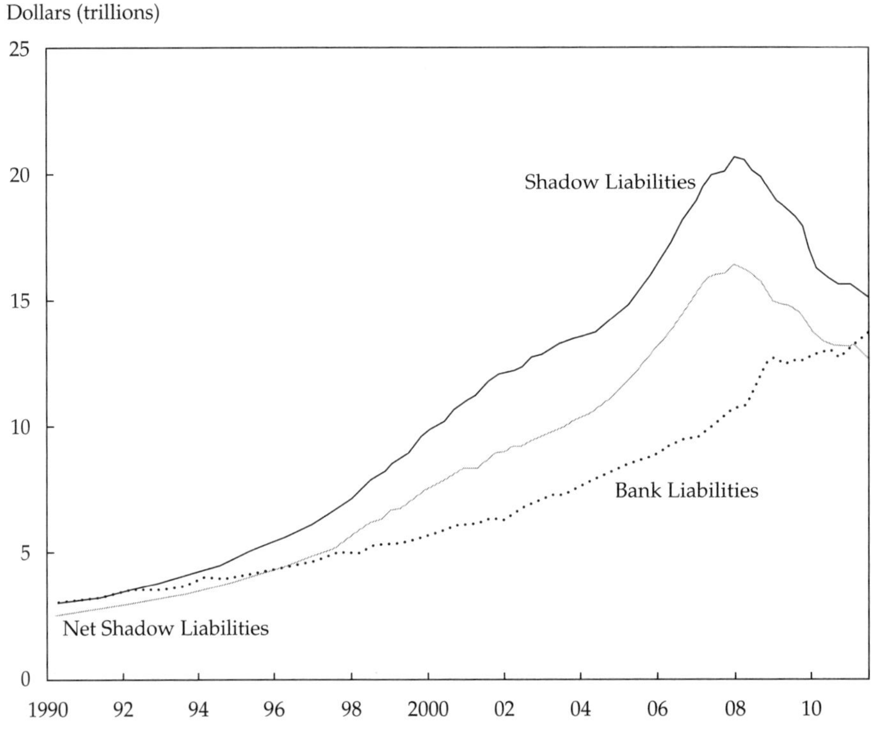

Sources: Pozsar, Adrian, Ashcraft, and Boesky (2010, p. 8), based on Fed flow of funds data.

Despite the fact that the shadow banking system overshadowed the traditional banking system in size, it did not receive comparable attention from economists or even much attention at all. Even as of mid-2014, there were only 25 academic papers on the Social Science Research Network (SSRN) devoted to structured investment vehicles, a key feature of this system. In fact, as of mid-2014, there were only 262 papers, according to SSRN, on "shadow banking" (using this as a search term). In contrast, there were 685 papers on

---

[57]Federal Reserve Bank of New York, based on Fed flow of funds data calculated in 2013.

"overconfidence," a behavioral concept related to subjects overestimating the precision of their knowledge (Fischhoff, Slovic, and Lichtenstein 1977).

This disparity in the number of research papers reflects the concerns of academic economists and journals during the many years leading up to the crash when behavioral concepts were most in vogue. Ironically, the behavioral research program on overconfidence is focused on the poor performance of naive day traders and corporate managers, not on the economics profession itself and economists' beliefs about their own level of understanding.

Nonetheless, the behavioral idea of overconfidence plays only a very minor role in the failure of macroeconomists and financial economists to fully consider the consequences of the transformation of the US financial system from one where sources of funding were insured deposits (by the FDIC) to one where short-term wholesale funding had no such government guarantees. Instead, as the SSRN results show, macroeconomists and financial economists were not interested in shadow banking, found it boring, or were completely unaware of it. Theory ruled out the importance of the financial sector, which was merely a veil. The lack of empirical papers on shadow banking is the practical manifestation of this theoretical void.

For those actually engaged in shadow banking, there was a widespread presumption that this system was inherently stable. After all, the system had many private mechanisms that provided guarantees. These ranged from expected and implicit support of bank sponsors of special purpose entities to the fact that borrowing was collateralized to tail risk insurance, such as credit default swaps.

In hindsight, these private sector guarantees failed to provide financial stability when the crisis hit. According to Pozsar, Adrian, Ashcraft, and Boesky (2010),

> The failure of private sector guarantees to support the shadow banking system occurred mainly because the relevant parties—credit rating agencies, risk managers, investors, and regulators—underestimated the aggregate risk and asset price correlations. Specifically, the market did not correctly price for the fact that valuations of highly rated structured securities become much more correlated in extreme environments than during normal times. (p. 3)

The shadow banking system, in effect, did not consider that it might itself be unstable or systemically risky. Instead, it viewed risk through the more myopic lens of VaR metrics or volatility, as well as ratings from the credit-rating agencies (which were paid for by the security issuers themselves). This combination of factors led to a huge expansion of credit during the great moderation. The narrowness of the approaches used for measuring risk has also been a key driver of the financial cycle discussed in Chapter 1.

As Pozsar et al. (2010) put it,

The emergence of shadow banking thus shifted the systemic risk–return trade-off toward cheaper credit intermediation during booms, at the cost of more severe crises and more expensive intermediation during downturns. (p. 2)

The 2007–09 crisis had all the hallmarks of a bank run, but the run was within the shadow banking system. The run stopped through the intervention of the Federal Reserve and its liquidity facilities and credit guarantees. There is still fierce debate and uncertainty about the exact mechanics of the acute stage of the crisis, such as where exactly the run first occurred and in what historical sequence it occurred.

Which Runs? This overview highlights some of the structural vulnerability of the shadow banking system in terms of its susceptibility to runs in short-term wholesale funding. Again, the system lacked a true liquidity backstop for this funding, in contrast to deposit insurance for retail funding, which largely prevented retail runs in the United States since the banking crisis of the 1930s.

The US financial system had many other vulnerabilities, only some of which are listed here, including perverse incentives for bankers favoring the short term over the long term. This asymmetric payoff for risk taking could negatively influence behavior and contribute to ethical lapses. Poor incentives might also help explain some of the failures of the credit-rating agencies. The intellectual limitations of their credit models—namely, their inability to grapple with correlational issues—must also be considered.

The spark that led to the fire sale in this highly vulnerable system came from the US housing market.[58] There is little disagreement that as early as 2006, there was an uptick in defaults and delinquencies of subprime mortgages originating that year (Federal Reserve Bank of St. Louis 2008). Also not in dispute among both researchers and regulators is that this decline in the credit quality of mortgage-related assets led to a sort of run in debt markets. But where this run first occurred is in dispute.

The dominant narrative in academia as well as much of the sophisticated financial press is to focus on the run on repo as central to the crisis and in many ways synonymous with it. Though this narrative is persuasive, more recent evidence points elsewhere, to runs in other markets that occurred prior to the repo market's problems.

Repo is short for repurchase agreement, a type of short-term loan from, for example, a money market fund to a broker/dealer. Lenders (depositors) receive collateral, such as mortgage-backed securities. The repo is a key source

---

[58]The practices in US mortgage finance, and US subprime in particular, deserve their own book. Suffice it to say that whereas margin trading in equities was tightly regulated and capped in the United States, leveraged purchasing of homes (a high loan-to-value ratio) was actively encouraged by US housing policy. For more on this topic, see Morgenson and Rosner's (2011) *Reckless Endangerment*.

of liquidity for the shadow banking system in general and broker/dealers in particular.[59]

The argument that the 2007–09 crisis was at its core a run on repo has been articulated most forcefully by Yale economist Gary Gorton. The stark conclusion of Gorton's (2010) book *Slapped by the Invisible Hand: The Panic of 2007* and his related papers is that "the panic of 2007–2008 was a run on the sale and repurchase market (the 'repo' market)" (Gorton and Metrick 2010, abstract).

When Gorton first unveiled his repo arguments at the 2008 Jackson Hole Conference of the Federal Reserve Bank of Kansas City, they were well in advance of conventional conceptualizations of the crisis at the time. Instead, according to Gorton (2010), conference participants largely blamed misaligned incentives in securitization as the culprit. The popular press mostly blamed bankers for the crisis, for gaming the system. Gorton himself blamed these misguided and superficial explanations on "the lack of visibility of the core aspect of the crisis—the run on the repo" (2010, p. 10).

The "run on repo" argument centers on the fact that repo transactions can be collateralized with securitized bonds. That is, the value of collateral used in repo is critical to the functioning of these markets. In a non-crisis state, the collateral can be easily valued and sold. During the subprime crisis, this was no longer the case for mortgage-backed assets used as collateral. According to Gorton, "Concerns about the liquidity of markets for the bonds used as collateral led to increases in repo 'haircuts': the amount of collateral required for any given transaction" (2010, p. 47). Repo haircuts spiked. He found that eventually, there was a cessation of repo lending against certain types of collateral altogether, a sort of run on the repo market.

This story makes intuitive sense: A collapse in or uncertainty about the value of mortgage-backed securities used as collateral caused a freezing up of repo markets, leading to illiquidity and eventual insolvency for the shadow banking system.

But even though the repo market encountered problems, this fact does not mean repo was central to the crisis, nor does it mean repo was the first market to experience a run. Indeed, there was a run in the shadow banking system and a crisis in short-term funding, but in all likelihood, they first occurred not in the repo market but in asset-backed commercial paper. ABCP had greater exposure to mortgage- or asset-backed securities than did repo; 4% of private-label asset-backed securities were directed to the repo market, whereas the comparative figure for ABCP is 23% (Krishnamurthy, Nagel, and Orlov forthcoming).[60]

---

[59]For more about repo and the differences between the trilateral repo market and the interdealer (bilateral) market, see Krishnamurthy, Nagel, and Orlov (Forthcoming).

[60]There is no single data source for the total composition of assets within ABCP portfolios.

The run in ABCP occurred well in advance of any problems in the repo market, as early as August 2007. It was also of comparatively greater magnitude than the decline in repo. From the second quarter of 2007 to the second quarter of 2009, the amount of ABCP outstanding contracted by $662 billion, compared with $182 billion for repo during this time (Krishnamurthy et al. forthcoming).

ABCP is similar to repo in that it involves asset-backed lending without government-provided deposit insurance. However, ABCP is much more complex than repo, because of the conduit structure that issues short-term debt, akin to a bank. Examining how different ABCP "programs'" behaved in late 2007 reveals a great deal about the sequence of the unfolding of the crisis sparked by the problems in the subprime market.

ABCP programs with high exposure to subprime assets experienced the clearest signs of a run in 2007. But there were signs of a panic across the entire ABCP market, not just in these programs. Covitz, Liang, and Suarez (2013) found "compelling evidence that runs in August and September 2007 had an important indiscriminate element" (p. 21). In effect, investors, unsure exactly what assets were held inside conduits and where exactly the bad assets lay, ran from ABCP. In August 2007, nearly a third of ABCP programs were in a run.[61]

This was not the end of the story. Money market mutual funds are a major investor in ABCP. They are low-return and, traditionally, low-risk investments, usually viewed as almost as safe as cash. But they are not completely safe: Unlike FDIC-insured bank deposits, they lack an explicit government guarantee. Their lack of complete safety became apparent in August 2007, when BNP Paribas stopped redemption from three money market funds. According to the bank, the unfolding crisis in mortgage-backed securities made it "impossible to value certain assets fairly regardless of their quality or credit rating."[62]

Even more dramatically, in the week following the collapse of Lehman Brothers, the Reserve Primary Fund, which held Lehman Brothers paper, "broke the buck" and experienced a run. Within days, investors ran from other money market funds to those with Treasury-only holdings (Kacperczyk and Schnabl 2013). Interestingly, the safest holdings of the money market fund sector were in tri-party repo, where most of the collateral was made up of Treasuries.

Repo still played a role in the downfall of the broker/dealer banks, such as Lehman Brothers, which relied on this market for their financing needs. (The time frame for the data used in the academic papers mentioned to analyze ABCP predates the fall of the broker/dealer banks, and hence, those papers

---

[61]Covitz et al.'s (2013) definition of a run is a program that "does not issue new paper during a week despite having a substantial share of its outstandings scheduled to mature" (p. 1).

[62]BNP Paribas, press release (9 August 2007): www.bnpparibas.com/en/news/press-release/bnp-paribas-investment-partners-temporaly-suspends-calculation-net-asset-value-fo.

do not shed much light on the mechanics of that story.) But the problems in ABCP predated and dwarfed those in repo.[63]

Eventually, the runs in these various markets ended through the interventions of the Fed, which provided liquidity backstops. The Fed's Asset-Backed Commercial Paper Money Market Mutual Fund Liquidity Facility, or AMLF, created a market for commercial paper. The runs ended, but at a cost: The risks of the $3 trillion money market were now borne by the US government.

Overall, this first intervention by the Fed was a huge success and deserves greater popular acknowledgement. If there is anything the government did wisely during the darkest days of the crisis, it was ending the massive runs on money market mutual funds through the explicit support the Fed provided. This does not make subsequent interventions wise or unwise; each must be evaluated on its own merits.

A Look Ahead

This ongoing debate about the exact sequence of runs in the crisis may seem academic today. But it shows how hard it remains to understand the complete details and nuances of the crisis. Aside from a few exceptions, such as the researchers mentioned in the previous section who actually studied the shadow banking system, most economists lacked a deep understanding of the architecture of this system and the markets involved in the crisis because of economics' lack of interest in shadow banking, in particular, and in financial frictions, in general, at least before the crisis.

Looking to the future, the key concern of policymakers and central bankers is how to build a more stable financial system, one that is more resilient to a shock. Today's preferred buzzword for reform is *macroprudential*, pertaining to the policies discussed in the previous chapter. That chapter laid out some of the theory behind macroprudential policy as well as some specific regulatory responses. In this section, I will look more closely at the practicalities and issues surrounding implementation. Will macroprudential policies, as currently constructed, truly create a financial system resilient enough to avoid a future crisis? What else could be done?

Implementation of policies deemed "macroprudential" has been very slow. An IMF study, "Not Making the Grade: Report Card on Global Financial Reform" (the study did not issue an actual grade), found that "reforms have yet to effect a safer set of structures" (Kodres 2012). It singled out too big to fail, concentration of bank assets, and domestic interbank linkages as unresolved global issues. The

---

[63]Repo markets consist of both money-market-fund-to-dealer repo and interdealer repo (lending among investment banks themselves). The sharpest rise in haircuts was in the latter market. Krishnamurthy et al.'s interpretation of this disparity is that "overall the problems in the repo market look less like the analogue of a traditional bank run by depositors and more like a credit crunch" (forthcoming, p.37).

report presents a picture of a financial sector that remains largely unreformed, at least along these dimensions, in most countries. *Macroprudential* seems to be more of a buzzword—a sign of good intentions or even good public relations—than an accurate description of today's dominant financial architecture, as evidenced by a substantially transformed financial system.

Whether today's hoped-for macroprudential reforms, even if they are somehow implemented, would be enough to truly mitigate systemic risk is an open question. Would they really work?

Macroprudential policies face the problem of regulatory arbitrage. Financial institutions could simply move their activities outside the "regulatory perimeter" to avoid burdensome regulation. Regulatory arbitrage can take many other forms. Suppose hedge funds become tightly regulated and reduce activities that are deemed to contribute to systemic risk. Insurance companies, for example, could use this opening to evolve into something more like hedge funds, even if they were still called "insurance companies" and were regulated as such. The financial sector can only be expected to innovate in the face of any macroprudential regulation.

Macroprudential policies face another risk: that risks they are trying to regulate will mutate, taking new, unanticipated forms. New types of crisis-producing mechanisms will appear. Current macroprudential efforts to ensure financial stability are in a sense backward looking: They are designed to address the last crisis, not the next one. Analogously, previous efforts at financial reform, such as the banking acts that came out of the Great Depression or "Regulation T" governing the margin requirements for stocks, were useful for addressing older crises but did not precisely target the risks in the shadow banking system in 2007–2009. As financial intermediation keeps changing, systemic risks keep changing; the current macroprudential toolkit will become anachronistic.

Finally, macroprudential policies are narrowly focused on the financial sector. They typically do not consider risks in the real economy, such as the housing boom that preceded the crisis in the United States and some other countries. They have not created a framework to incorporate regulation addressing these "real risks" into their financial sector reforms.

These uncertainties about macroprudential policies—whether they will ever be implemented and, if they are, whether they will be effective—have set off a fierce debate among central bankers. The debate is complex but centers on the objectives for monetary policy as well as its proper role. At the core of the debate is whether monetary policy should consider macroprudential objectives in addition to its traditional objectives of price stability and, sometimes, full employment.

That is, should monetary policy be used to achieve financial stability by leaning against growing systemic risks? Or, alternatively, should monetary policy ignore perceived systemic risks as long as these risks are not immediately affecting employment or inflation? Here, the argument would be that financial stability is best accomplished through macroprudential regulation and related supervision alone rather than interest rate policy.

Central bankers fall into different camps on this issue. For example, a 2009 Bank of England discussion paper, "The Role of Macroprudential Policy," argued that monetary policy and macroprudential policy have distinct roles and objectives. "The goal of monetary policy is to stabilize the aggregate price of goods" (BOE 2009, p. 10), whereas the macroprudential goal is to ensure the resilience of the financial system. Though these objectives can be complementary, they can also work at cross-purposes. For example, according to the paper, if monetary policy were used as a tool to reduce the rapid growth of bank balance sheets during the Great Moderation, it could have destabilized the real economy.

A counterfactual exercise developed in BOE (2009) shows just how destabilizing and damaging it would be to the real economy if short-term interest rates were used as a macroprudential tool. If the objective were to reduce credit growth and bank balance sheets, interest rates would have to be set much higher than they would using the Taylor rule, which primarily seeks to limit inflation. These high short-term interest rates would lead to aggregate losses in output and employment, which BOE (2009) terms "large" (no numbers are provided for this counterfactual exercise).

In short, according to this camp of central bankers, monetary policy is too blunt a tool to use for reducing rising systemic risks. Instead, policymakers should rely on macroprudential regulation and tools not related to interest rates, such as countercyclical capital buffers that precisely target systemic risks.

In a 2014 speech, Harvard professor Jeremy Stein, who was at the time a Federal Reserve governor, made the opposite case. He argued that financial stability concerns should be part of a monetary policy framework and should influence actual monetary policy decisions. Stein (2014) stated that "all else being equal, monetary policy should be less accommodative" when there are signs of growing financial market vulnerability.[64] Stein's (2014) argument rests on the idea that "financial market vulnerability may not be easily addressed by supervision and regulation." In other words, macroprudential tools and regulation cannot get into every nook and cranny of risk taking. Only an increase in interest rates can truly dampen growing systemic risks.

---

[64]Stein uses an unusual measure of a financial system's vulnerability. He does not use the standard measure of the BIS, the credit-to-GDP gap. As Stein (2014) pointed out, it remains unclear how monetary policy influences the credit-to-GDP gap. Instead, his hypothetical trigger for tightening is the high-yield issuance share. This is a predictive measure of bond market overheating developed by Greenwood and Hanson (2013).

The last word in this debate should go to the first speaker: Irving Fisher. Recall that his theory of the Great Depression included an analysis of the boom that preceded it. The "bad actor" in this boom was over-indebtedness. Fisher pinpointed the origin of what he called the "debt disease." Fisher wrote, "Easy money is the great cause of over borrowing" (1933, p. 348).

Though Fisher might not have used this language, monetary policy must at least take into account considerations of financial stability, even if there is, as of yet, no precise quantitative guidance on how best to do this. Macroprudential tools will still be required to work in tandem with monetary policy to ensure stability, but monetary policy cannot be held blameless for an overheating financial system.

Current Interventions

These debates among central bankers and macroprudential reformers, centered on the best ways to improve the resilience of the financial system and the proper objectives for monetary policy, are almost exclusively forward looking. Their obsession with preventing the next crisis neglects a more immediate issue: how to best fully recover from the crisis of 2007–2009 and its legacy of macro and financial instability.

This issue is far from resolved, and there is evidence that some of the interventions taken during and after the 2007–09 crisis were nonproductive or even counterproductive. The consequences go far beyond the moral hazard created by such interventions.

The bank bailouts undertaken by eurozone periphery countries are a case in point. For example, in 2008, Ireland guaranteed the deposits of its troubled large banks. Once this occurred, the credit default swap (CDS) rate for these banks immediately fell from 400 bps to 150 bps. But over time, the CDS rate for sovereign credit risk of the government of Ireland itself rose, eventually reaching 400 bps, an exact offset of the banking sector risk before the intervention (Acharya, Drechsler, and Schnabl 2011). In Ireland, the risk in the banking sector was merely transferred to the sovereign, not eliminated.

Acharya et al. (2011) modeled how a government's bailouts of a financial sector lead to an offsetting increase in sovereign credit risk, which, in turn, can damage banks that hold this downgraded sovereign debt. This creates a negative feedback loop resulting from the initial bailout. According to Acharya et al. (2011),

> Bailout costs are not just in the future. They are priced into the sovereign's credit risk and cost of borrowing, and weaken the financial sector further. Thus, aggressive bailout packages that stabilize financial sectors can end up being a Pyrrhic victory. (p. 1)

Extremely accommodative monetary policies after a crisis can similarly produce Pyrrhic victories. The argument here, put forward most vocally by the BIS, but also put forward by others,[65] is that ultralow interest rates during the recovery phase of a financial crisis can lead to misallocation of credit and ultimately of real resources. The reason is that low interest rates keep "zombie" banks and nonfinancial firms alive. (A zombie bank or firm is one that would go out of business if it lacked support by government or creditors.) Investment keeps flows going to these firms and sectors rather than to more productive sectors.

Japan is a case in point. Japanese banks, during the lost decade of the 1990s after that country's financial crisis, preferred to continue to extend credit to underperforming firms rather than to more productive firms. Otherwise, they would have to recognize losses on these bad loans (Peek and Rosengren 2005). Investment in productive sectors was comparatively hindered. Ultralow interest rates, therefore, result in a distorted economy, one slow to recover from a financial crash.

The central post-crisis policy problem is how to resolve the "debt overhang" created by the financial crash and the bottoming out of the financial cycle. The financial system and the real economy have to pay off debts accumulated during the boom period of the cycle. Debt overhangs are associated with a reduction in investment (Myers 1977) because any proceeds from new investments must be used to pay off creditors, not the new investors.

This debt overhang is present in the balance sheets of firms, households, and governments after a financial crisis; hence, recessions following these crises are often deemed "balance sheet recessions" (Koo 2013, BIS 2014). As discussed in Chapter 1, recessions stemming from a financial crisis are much worse and longer than conventional recessions. Credit delivery to the real economy is disrupted during the acute phase of the crisis itself, as captured in macro amplification models. But even beyond this initial disruption, the debt overhang needs to be dealt with and balance sheets need to be repaired after the crisis, further hindering growth.

There are many policy experiments underway to speed the recovery from the financial crisis, too many for this book to track or even categorize. Some are Keynesian or demand driven in nature, others use monetary tools, and others directly focus on debt restructuring. The success story in this last category was the response to the Nordic banking crisis of the 1990s. Following that crisis, policymakers in the Nordic countries forced banks to recognize losses. They also recapitalized banks. Balance sheets of banks were, hence, quickly repaired, leading to a sustained recovery.[66]

---

[65]See Caruana (2012). There are many papers about zombie lending and the slow recovery in Japan. See Hoshi and Kashyap (2010, 2013); Caballero, Hoshi, and Kashyap (2008).
[66]Borio, Vale, and von Peter (2010).

There are other ways to eliminate a debt overhang. Aggressively inflating away debts is, of course, a possibility, but it is not one policymakers are rushing to embrace. Irving Fisher himself argued that "reflation" was the way to end a Great Depression stemming from a debt-deflation cycle.

More common are fiscal or monetary policies that seek to foster a recovery after a crisis. Though both can be effective during the acute phase of a crisis, by reducing uncertainty, are they the right tools for the post-crisis recovery phase?[67] This is a controversial question. There is reason to worry about "overburdening" monetary policy with the additional responsibility of recovering from crashes.

The concern goes beyond the conventional ones—that monetary policy could be ineffective because it will be constrained by the zero lower bound for nominal interest rates or, alternatively, because it could set off inflation in the future. Rather, the problem is that extremely accommodative monetary policy after a crash could further the distortions of the economy by keeping zombie banks and companies alive, as in the case of Japan. Low rates, instead of reviving the real economy, could instead add to financial fragility and a widening of the credit-to-GDP gap.

The BIS, a central bank hyper-vigilant about growth in credit, contends that monetary and fiscal policies eventually become ineffective at restoring economies to a sustainable growth path during a balance sheet recession. Claudio Borio, an economist at the BIS, in a working paper about central banking after the crisis, highlighted

> the collateral damage of such an accommodative stance if kept beyond the crisis management phase. After all, if the origin of the problem was too much debt, how can a policy that encourages the private and public sectors to accumulate more debt be part of the solution? (Borio 2011, p. 4)[68]

Borio, however, in this same working paper, admitted that there is no "agreement on the proper role of monetary policy in the aftermath of a financial crisis" (2011, p. 4).

A reason for this lack of agreement on how to best resolve a debt overhang and recover from a balance sheet recession comes back to theory. There is not much macroeconomic theory dealing with this issue. There are many opinions and real-world policy experiments, but actual theory in this area is, if anything,

---

[67]Interest rate cuts, however, may actually be damaging in the middle of a liquidity spiral. Ashcroft, Gârleanu, and Pedersen (2010) showed in a model that interest rate cuts are counterproductive when leveraged agents hit their margin constraints, which occurs in a liquidity spiral. The reason is that the cuts increase the required returns for high-margin assets. A reduction in haircuts is a much more effective tool during a spiral, which effectively occurred when the Fed introduced the Term Asset-Backed Securities Loan Facility, or TALF.

[68]Borio's quote is very similar in spirit to Hayek's argument that monetary stimulus was not a useful tool during a depression: "To combat the depression by a forced credit expansion is to attempt to cure the evil by the very means which brought it about" (Hayek 1933).

weaker and less developed than that dealing with systemic risk. It is fragmentary, even elusive, and remains on the frontier of modeling.

The issue of debt overhang is completely missing from a frictionless framework because it involves a friction: the renegotiation of debt. At the same time, current macro friction models, described in Chapter 1, also do not directly model how to resolve a debt overhang. They are not designed to be used for quantitative policy evaluations regarding this issue. Instead, they are more concerned with modeling amplification mechanisms of how a small shock can be magnified into something much larger through the involvement of the financial sector. A Keynesian analysis suggests a policy conclusion, though this analysis also does not explicitly model a debt overhang.

There are some academic papers with a narrower focus on dealing with debt overhang in the household sector. Mian and Sufi's work on household balance sheets is far in advance of most of the literature because it tightly captures the problem and also proposes solutions. But for the moment, there is no canonical macro friction model of how to resolve a debt overhang or balance sheet recession.

Perhaps such a model will come next in friction theory; just as friction modelers struggled with and were eventually able to model the ferocity of a financial crash, they may next be able to model how to recover from one.

Secular Stagnation: Long-Term Problem or Temporary Condition?

It is still a matter of much dispute among economists why growth since the crisis has been so painfully slow. Perhaps the most prominent view, put forward by the Harvard professor and former US Treasury Secretary Larry Summers, is that the advanced economies have entered a period of "secular stagnation." This term was first introduced by the economist Alvin Hansen in 1938 to describe the US economy's inability to emerge from the Great Depression. Today, a common definition of "secstag," as it is known, is that "negative real interest rates are needed to equate saving and investment with full employment" (Teulings and Baldwin 2014, p. 2). Summer's articulation of his hypothesis is that a decline in the full-employment real interest rate and low inflation have together created conditions where "it may be impossible for an economy to achieve full employment, satisfactory growth, and financial stability simultaneously simply through the operation of conventional monetary policy" (Teulings and Baldwin 2014, p. 2). As a result, actual growth is below potential. Other authors, such as the Northwestern University professor Robert Gordon, claim that long-term potential growth itself has declined because of slow technological progress and "structural headwinds" (Teulings and Baldwin 2014). Observers have proposed many other reasons why growth has been so slow, including reduced incentives to participate in the labor force in the United States and elsewhere as well as the global lack of safe financial assets.[69]

Secstag analyses may vary widely, but a general (though not unanimous) theme, according to Barry Eichengreen, is that "America and the other advanced economies might be suffering from more than the hangover from a financial crisis" (Teulings and Baldwin 2014, p. 3).

This book, however, takes a different point of view: that the currently weak rate of growth primarily stems from the devastation caused by the financial crisis itself, and from the post-crisis debt overhang in the real economy. After all, Reinhart and Rogoff (2009) found that slow recovery was a standard feature of post-crisis recessions throughout the world. Muir's (2014) analysis, discussed earlier in the book, also pointed to the unique economic damage caused by financial crises, which, in some respects, is even worse than the economic fallout from a war.

It is possible that advanced economies are grappling with, in addition to the unusual stresses stemming from the financial crisis, an unrelated problem of secular stagnation and diminishing rates of technological advance—maybe. But it is also possible that slow growth in the advanced economies stems from the pre-crisis boom itself. The boom in the United States, as was seen in peripheral countries like Portugal or Greece, may have misallocated resources to slow-growth, consumption-heavy sectors, such as housing, and away from the tradable sector, damaging productivity.

Standard secstag policy solutions attempt to find ways to cope with the zero-lower-bound problem or favor fiscal expansion to increase demand.

Theory remains very underdeveloped in this area, and the results of ongoing policy experiments are still unknown. But the aftermath of the financial crisis—if it is the actual cause of secstag—calls for a different type of policy response. A focus on frictions suggests that the most effective approach for ending a balance sheet recession is to directly target the friction causing the recession—the debt overhang itself. This can be accomplished through writing off debt of both households and banks and recapitalizing banks.[70]

More conventional Keynesian policies do not target the problem as precisely. Moreover, as secstag proponents are the first to admit, conventional monetary policy may not work at all right now, at least not without the risk

---

[69]For an anthology of secstag analysis by different contributors, see Teulings and Baldwin (2014). These essays generally avoid contemplating debt restructuring as a solution, perhaps indicating that there are taboos in conventional policy analysis.

[70]Not every economist who believes the current slow growth is primarily a balance sheet recession, caused by the effects of deleveraging, calls for a write-down of debts. Richard Koo (2013), who falls into this camp and indeed pioneered it (and also sees secstag as synonymous with a balance sheet recession), argues that a fiscal policy response is more urgent. See also Teulings and Baldwin (2014).

of increased financial instability. Post-crisis policies typically try to address a symptom of the recession—high unemployment—but not the true cause: damaged balance sheets of financial institutions and households.

"Rescheduling" or writing off debt is a highly unsettling topic, involving grave issues of fairness. It is not fair to place the burden of ending debt overhangs entirely on the back of creditors. Doing so could break their backs, to continue the metaphor, and risks setting off global negative feedback loops. Also, it would result in higher rates for borrowers in the future, a far from ideal outcome.

The Nordic debt write-off and recapitalization of banks is an example of a successful solution for a balance sheet recession. (In contrast, the US "cash for clunkers" program is an example of an unsuccessful, wide of the mark, and, ultimately, bizarre intervention in response to a post-crisis recession.)[71] The Nordic approach directly targeted the causative friction—the problem of debt overhang and related credit constraints—rather than just the symptoms of the recession. In contrast to ineffective Keynesian or monetarist policies, the Nordic recapitalization led to a speedy and robust recovery from a balance sheet recession.

Conclusion

> Friction is the only concept that more or less corresponds to the factors that distinguish real war from war on paper.
>
> —Clausewitz, *On War*

Economic Blindness to Financial Frictions. The sciences, such as physics, have long acknowledged the importance of frictions. Physics has been exploring frictions since the experiments of Leonardo da Vinci and Galileo. Friction explains why a pound of feathers falls to earth more slowly than a pound of gold. Math contemplates frictions. Even the war theorist Clausewitz thought about frictions, as seen in the epigraph.

The question remains why macroeconomics and financial economics, unlike other sciences or social sciences, have put so little effort into investigating frictions. (Economics does model some frictions, such as search costs. Also, sticky wages and prices are central to new Keynesian models, but they are lacking from new classical models.) This intellectual failure occurs partly because certain threads of economic theory—incorrectly, we now see—ruled out the importance of financial frictions. But the argument put forward throughout this book is that the failure to contemplate financial frictions also stemmed from historical conditions. Financial frictions were not particularly obvious

---

[71]*Clunker* is US slang for a used car in poor condition.

or relevant during the post–World War II period in the United States, when many of the canonical models in economics and finance were developed. This was a period of financial stability in the United States, though not, of course, in many other countries.

There is another reason why economics has ignored financial frictions, which relates to the historical development of economics itself and its modeling objectives. When it comes to economic models, most of the focus and energy has been on the modeling, not the economics. Models that are computationally tractable have been favored over models that incorporate the messy details of the real world. DSGE models are a case in point. In these models, all agents are creditworthy. There is no money. There are no financial intermediaries. These models may lack these critical empirical details that are central to financial crises, but they are formally elegant, which seems to have been an end in itself.

This is underscored by an observation of William White, chief economist of the OECD, about DSGE models' actual forecasting abilities, which appear to have been only a remote concern for the macroeconomists involved in developing them. White wrote, "Little effort was made to evaluate the forecasting capacity of these models, either in- or out-of-sample" (2013, p. 13).

The way math is used in economics modeling is representative of this strange lack of real-world interest and may be a contributor to it. The mathematization of economics is not necessarily the problem here; math has dramatically increased the analytical power of economics. But math is deployed differently in economic modeling than in physics, a field that economics both emulates and envies. "The kind of mathematics used in economics is typically that of the department of mathematics, not that of the departments of physics or of engineering," wrote the economist and economic historian Deirdre McCloskey. McCloskey, who is interested in the rhetoric of economics, added, "Physics is finding driven. Economics is proof driven" (1994, p. 131). Economists, according to McCloskey, are in this sense misguided about what science actually involves.

McCloskey took this point even further. She argued that economics resembles a "cargo cult science." This term was coined by the physicist Richard Feynman, referencing South Pacific islanders who built mock airports to attract real (American) planes that they hoped would deliver real cargo resembling that which they had seen when US soldiers visited the islands years before. Cargo cult sciences are similarly mock or pretend sciences, which replicate the form of a science but not the substance. McCloskey (2005) argued that this describes economics: It "looked like science, had all that hard math and statistics, plenty of long words; but actual science, actual inquiry into the world, was not going on." This description of economics is harsh and mostly wrong. Yet, it was uncannily true in describing the field's lack of interest in shadow banking in the years before the crash.

Perceiving Frictions. Adding frictions to economic models changes the mathematical equation. Suddenly, economic modeling is very interested in the real world and is able to generate new insights that apply to it. The way the new models are constructed is still very traditional: Friction modeling is still proof driven, like the rest of economics. But it is also finding driven, like physics. Because of this hybridity, friction models are acceptable to the core of the profession, while shifting the modeling focus to topics where frictions have a lot to add, such as in the working of financial markets or the macroeconomy. The study of frictions is not a radical field. Unlike heterodox economics or the work of certain followers of Minsky, friction theory does not propose that contemporary economics be demolished. Rather, it is rebuilding economics along new lines that take into account the real world.

This effort to add financial frictions is mostly a work in progress. There is still a lot of work to be done. Friction theory still needs to provide better guidance for monetary policy in terms of preventing a financial crash as well as how to best recover from one. It also needs to provide asset pricing models that are more tractable than the L-CAPM and that more explicitly incorporate concepts of funding liquidity. Macro friction models should develop beyond just modeling the mechanics of the bust, to include the endogenous credit boom that preceded it and more detail about the household and corporate sectors. Fully exploring the link between government intervention and financial sector risk is the big unknown. There is a distinct possibility that the macro stabilizing policies used to alleviate recessions during the Great Moderation contributed to the buildup of the financial cycle that culminated in the financial crisis and the severe recession that followed.

This will all take time. It will be a long time before such concepts as the financial cycle trickle down to financial planning and investment management. How to optimally build portfolios in a time of ongoing financial instability will demand new metrics and guidance, particularly along dimensions of liquidity and liquidity risk. Standard risk management practices will have to broaden.

Though financial friction theory is not yet in a stage of theoretical completeness like the economics that preceded it, it has already had enormous breakthroughs. It explains why financial crises are uniquely dire. It explains why price stability is no guarantee of financial or macro stability. It suggests that central bankers and investors need to look beyond conventional economic indicators—such as inflation, volatility, and expectations—and instead focus on credit growth. Friction theory has drafted new policy ideas, such as the usefulness of capital controls. It has found new ways to measure systemic risk and maybe even mitigate it. It has created new approaches to asset pricing—identifying new factors—and new ideas for portfolio design. It suggests that there is a tradeoff between credit-driven economic growth and financial stability, a tradeoff policymakers need to think about more carefully in the future. Ultimately, it has moved macroeconomics away from a theoretical dead-end, where macro models excluded financial frictions and the financial sector altogether.

Financial friction theory, as discussed in the Prologue, has not reached the state of a "classical situation." It is "on the boil," rather than in a state of repose. The new theory being constructed may not yet resemble "the finality of a Greek temple that spreads its perfect lines against a cloudless sky,"[72] as previous theory did. The temple of old theory, and its micro-foundations, however beautiful, excluded much that was important, and it turned out to be fragile in the end. The new edifice being erected is much more robust. Its theories and policies should be better able to withstand or even mitigate the next financial crisis when it inevitably arises.

---

[72]Schumpeter (1954, p. 754)

References

Acharya, Viral V., Yakov Amihud, and Sreedhar T. Bharath. 2010. "Liquidity Risk of Corporate Bond Returns: A Conditional Approach." NBER Working Paper 16394 (September).

Acharya, Viral V., Itamar Drechsler, and Philipp Schnabl. 2011. "A Pyrrhic Victory?—Bank Bailouts and Sovereign Credit Risk." NBER Working Paper 17136 (June).

Acharya, Viral V., and Lasse H. Pedersen. 2005. "Asset Pricing with Liquidity Risk." *Journal of Financial Economics*, vol. 77, no. 2 (August):375–410.

Acharya, Viral V., and Sascha Steffen. Forthcoming. "The Greatest Carry Trade Ever? Understanding Eurozone Bank Risks." *Journal of Financial Economics*.

Adler, David. 2009. *Snap Judgment*. Upper Saddle River, NJ: FT Press.

———. 2012. *The New Field of Liquidity and Financial Frictions*. Charlottesville, VA: CFA Institute Research Foundation (www.cfapubs.org/toc/rflr/2012/7/2).

Adrian, Tobias, and Markus K. Brunnermeier. 2011. "CoVaR." NBER Working Paper 17454 (October).

Adrian, Tobias, and Nina Boyarchenko. 2013. "Intermediary Balance Sheets." Federal Reserve Bank of New York Staff Report 651 (November): www.newyorkfed.org/research/staff_reports/sr651.html.

Adrian, Tobias, Paolo Colla, and Hyun Song Shin. 2012. "Which Financial Frictions? Parsing the Evidence from the Financial Crisis of 2007–09." Federal Reserve Bank of New York Staff Report 528 (June): www.newyorkfed.org/research/staff_reports/sr528.html.

Adrian, Tobias, Erkko Etula, and Tyler Muir. Forthcoming. "Financial Intermediaries and the Cross-Section of Asset Returns." *Journal of Finance*.

Adrian, Tobias, Erkko Etula, and Hyun Song Shin. 2009. "Risk Appetite and Exchange Rates." Federal Reserve Bank of New York Staff Report 361 (January): www.newyorkfed.org/research/staff_reports/sr361.pdf.

Adrian, Tobias, Emanuel Moench, and Hyun Song Shin. 2013. "Dynamic Leverage Asset Pricing." Federal Reserve Bank of New York Staff Report 625 (August): www.newyorkfed.org/research/staff_reports/sr625.pdf.

Adrian, Tobias, and Hyun Song Shin. 2008. "Liquidity and Financial Contagion." *Financial Stability Review* (Banque de France), special issue on liquidity, no. 11 (February): 1–7 (www.banque-france.fr/fileadmin/user_upload/banque_de_france/publications/Revue_de_la_stabilite_financiere/rsf_0208.pdf).

———. 2010. "The Changing Nature of Financial Intermediation and the Financial Crisis of 2007–2009." *Annual Review of Economics*, vol. 2 (September):603–618.

————. 2011. "Financial Intermediary Balance Sheet Management." *Annual Review of Financial Economics*, vol. 3 (December):289–307.

————. 2013. "Procyclical Leverage and Value-at-Risk." *Review of Financial Studies* (www.newyorkfed.org/research/staff_reports/sr338.html).

Aikman, David, Andrew G. Haldane, and Benjamin D. Nelson. 2010. "Curbing the Credit Cycle." Paper prepared for the Columbia University Center on Capitalism and Society Annual Conference.

Amihud, Yakov, and Haim Mendelson. 1986. "Asset Pricing and the Bid–Ask Spread." *Journal of Financial Economics*, vol. 17, no. 2 (December):223–249.

Amihud, Yakov, Haim Mendelson, and Lasse H. Pedersen. 2013. *Market Liquidity Asset Pricing, Risk, and Crises*. New York: Cambridge University Press.

Arrow, Kenneth J., and Gérard Debreu. 1954. "Existence of an Equilibrium for a Competitive Economy." *Econometrica*, vol. 22, no. 3 (July):265–290.

Ashcroft, Adam, Nicolae Gârleanu, and Lasse Heje Pedersen. 2010. "Two Monetary Tools: Interest Rates and Haircuts." *NBER Macroeconomics Annual*, vol. 25, no. 1: 143–180.

Asness, Clifford, Andrea Frazzini, and Lasse H. Pedersen. 2012. "Leverage Aversion and Risk Parity." *Financial Analysts Journal*, vol. 68, no. 1 (January/February):47–59.

Barbera, Robert. 2009. *The Cost of Capitalism: Understanding Market Mayhem and Stabilizing Our Economic Future*. New York: McGraw-Hill.

Barberis, Nicholas, and Richard Thaler. 2003. "A Survey of Behavioral Finance." *Handbook of the Economics of Finance*. Edited by George Constantinides, René M. Stulz, and Milton Harris. Amsterdam: Elsevier.

Bernanke, Ben S. 2012. "Some Reflections on the Crisis and the Policy Response." Speech at the "Rethinking Finance: Perspectives on the Crisis" conference of the Russell Sage Foundation and the Century Foundation (13 April): www.federalreserve.gov/newsevents/speech/bernanke20120413a.pdf.

Bernanke, Ben S., and Mark Gertler. 1989. "Agency Costs, Net Worth, and Business Fluctuations." *American Economic Review*, vol. 79, no. 1 (March):14–31.

————. 1990. "Financial Fragility and Economic Performance." *Quarterly Journal of Economics*, vol. 105, no. 1 (February):87–114.

Bernanke, Ben S., Mark Gertler, and Simon Gilchrist. 1996. "The Financial Accelerator and the Flight to Quality." *Review of Economics and Statistics*, vol. 78, no. 1 (February):1–15.

————. 1999. "The Financial Accelerator in a Quantitative Business Cycle Framework." In *Handbook of Macroeconomics*, 1st ed., vol. 1. Edited by J.B. Taylor and M. Woodford. San Diego: Elsevier.

BIS. 2010. "Guidance for National Authorities Operating the Countercyclical Capital Buffer" (December): www.bis.org/publ/bcbs187.htm.

————. 2011. "Global Systemically Important Banks: Assessment Methodology and the Additional Loss Absorbency Requirement" (November): www.bis.org/publ/bcbs207cn.pdf.

————. 2014. "BIS 84th Annual Report, 2013/2014" (29 June).

Black, Fischer. 1972. "Capital Market Equilibrium with Restricted Borrowing." *Journal of Business*, vol. 45, no. 3 (July):444–455.

BOE. 2009. "The Role of Macroprudential Policy: A Discussion Paper" (November): www.bankofengland.co.uk/publications/Documents/other/financialstability/roleofmacroprudentialpolicy091121.pdf.

Borio, Claudio E. 2011. "Central Banking Post-Crisis: What Compass for Uncharted Waters?" BIS Working Paper 353 (1 September): www.bis.org/publ/work353.pdf.

————. 2012. "The Financial Cycle and Macroeconomics: What Have We Learnt?" BIS Working Paper 395 (December): www.bis.org/publ/work395.pdf.

Borio, Claudio E., and Mathias Drehmann. 2009. "Assessing the Risk of Banking Crises—Revisited." *BIS Quarterly Review* (March): 29–46: www.bis.org/publ/qtrpdf/r_qt0903e.pdf.

Borio, Claudio, Bent Vale, and Goetz von Peter. 2010. "Resolving the Financial Crisis: Are We Heeding the Lessons from the Nordics?" BIS Working Paper 311 (June): www.bis.org/publ/work311.pdf.

Breeden, Douglas. 1979. "An Intertemporal Asset Pricing Model with Stochastic Consumption and Investment Opportunities." *Journal of Financial Economics*, vol. 7, no. 3 (September):265–296.

Brunnermeier, Markus, and Lasse Heje Pedersen. 2009. "Market Liquidity and Funding Liquidity." *Review of Financial Studies*, vol. 22, no. 6 (June):2201–2238.

Brunnermeier, Markus, and Yuliy Sannikov. 2014. "A Macroeconomic Model with a Financial Sector." *American Economic Review*, vol. 104, no. 2 (February):379–421.

Bush, Oliver, Rodrigo Guimaraes, and Hanno Stremmel. 2013. "Beyond the Credit Gap: Quantity and Price of Risk Indicators for Macroprudential Policy." Presentation at Frontiers of Systemic Risk Forecasting Conference, London School of Economics (28 November): www.systemicrisk.ac.uk/sites/default/files/media/GuimaraesLSEpresentationNov13.pdf.

Caballero, Ricardo, Takeo Hoshi, and Anil K. Kashyap. 2008. "Zombie Lending and Depressed Restructuring in Japan." *American Economic Review*, vol. 98, no. 5 (December):1943–1977.

Calvo, Guillermo. 1998. "Capital Flows and Capital-Market Crises: The Simple Economics of Sudden Stops." *Journal of Applied Econometrics*, vol. 1, no. 1 (November):35–54.

Campbell, John Y., and John Cochrane. 1999. "By Force of Habit: A Consumption-Based Explanation of Aggregate Stock Market Behavior." *Journal of Political Economy*, vol. 107, no. 2 (April):205–251.

Caruana, Jaime. 2012. "International Monetary Policy Interactions: Challenges and Prospects." Speech delivered at the CEMLA-SEACEN conference "The Role of Central Banks in Macroeconomic and Financial Stability: The Challenges in an Uncertain and Volatile World" (16 November): www.bis.org/speeches/sp121116.htm.

Chen, Hui, Scott Joslin, and Sophie Ni. 2014. "Demand for Crash Insurance, Intermediary Constraints, and Stock Return Predictability." AFA 2013 San Diego Meetings Paper (March).

Claessens, S, M.A. Kose, and M.E. Terrones. 2011. "Financial Cycles: What? How? When?" IMF Working Paper WP/11/76 (www.imf.org/external/pubs/ft/wp/2011/wp1176.pdf).

Clement, Piet. 2010. "The Term 'Macroprudential': Origins and Evolution." *BIS Quarterly Review* (March).

Cochrane, John. 2011. "Presidential Address: Discount Rates." *Journal of Finance*, vol. 66, no. 4 (August):1047–1108.

Constâncio, Vítor. 2013. "The European Crisis and the Role of the Financial System." Speech at the Bank of Greece conference "The Crisis in the Euro Area" (23 May): www.ecb.europa.eu/press/key/date/2013/html/sp130523_1.en.html.

Corcoran, Terence. 2012. "Robert Mundell: Euro Is Here to Stay." *Financial Post* (8 June): http://opinion.financialpost.com/2012/06/08/robert-mundell-euro-is-here-to-stay.

Corsetti, Giancarlo. 2010. "The 'Original Sin' in the Eurozone." *VoxEU* (9 May): www.voxeu.org/article/eurozone-s-original-sin.

Covitz, Daniel M., Nellie Liang, and Gustavo Suarez. 2013. "The Evolution of a Financial Crisis: Collapse of the Asset-Backed Commercial Paper Market." *Journal of Finance*, vol. 68, no. 3 (June):815–848.

De Grauwe, Paul. 2013. "The European Central Bank as Lender of Last Resort in the Government Bond Markets." *CESifo Economic Studies*, vol. 59, no. 3 (September):520–535.

De la Torre, Augusto, and Alain Ize. 2009. "Containing Systemic Risk: Are Regulatory Reform Proposals on the Right Track?" World Bank Other Operational Studies 10967 (October 26).

DeRosa, David F. 2009. *Central Banking and Monetary Policy in Emerging-Markets Nations*. Charlottesville, VA: CFA Institute Research Foundation.

Diamond, Douglas W. 2009. "Lessons from the Credit Crisis." Presentation at the Philadelphia Fed Policy Forum (4 December): www.philadelphiafed.org/research-and-data/events/2009/fed-policy-forum/presentations/Diamond_2009%20Crisis%20Diamond%20phl_Revised.pdf.

Dominguez, Kathryn M., Ray C. Fair, and Matthew D. Shapiro. 1988. "Forecasting the Depression: Harvard versus Yale." *American Economic Review*, vol. 78, no. 4 (September):595–612 (www-personal.umich.edu/~kathrynd/files/16aer.forecastingthedepression.sep88.pdf).

Drehmann, Mathias, Claudio Borio, and Kostas Tsatsaronis. 2012. "Characterising the Financial Cycle: Do Not Lose Sight of the Medium Term!" BIS Working Paper 380 (June).

Drehmann, Mathias, and Kostas Tsatsaronis. 2014. "The Credit-to-GDP Gap and Countercyclical Capital Buffers: Questions and Answers." *BIS Quarterly Review* (March).

Duffie, Darrell. 2011. "Systemic Risk Exposures: A 10-by-10-by-10 Approach." NBER Working Paper 17281 (August).

Eatwell, John, and Murray Milgate. 2011. *The Fall and Rise of Keynesian Economics*. New York: Oxford University Press.

ECB. 2010. "Analytical Models and Tools for the Identification and Assessment of Systemic Risks." *Financial Stability Review* (European Central Bank, June): www.ecb.europa.eu/pub/pdf/other/financialstabilityreview201006en.pdf??e4a9882960473 1bb5628a660af1a756c.

Edge, Rochelle M., and Ralf R. Meisenzahl. 2011. "The Unreliability of Credit-to-GDP Ratio Gaps in Real Time: Implications for Countercyclical Capital Buffers." *International Journal of Central Banking* (December): www.ijcb.org/journal/ijcb11q4a10.htm.

Eichengreen, Barry, Ricardo Hausmann, and Ugo Panizza. 2005. "The Mystery of Original Sin." In *Other People's Money*. Edited by Barry Eichengreen and Ricardo Hausmann. Chicago: University of Chicago Press.

European Commission. 2013. "Taxation of the Financial Sector" (February): http://ec.europa.eu/taxation_customs/resources/documents/taxation/com_2013_71_en.pdf.

Federal Reserve Bank of St. Louis. 2008. "The Financial Crisis Timeline" (http://timeline.stlouisfed.org/index.cfm?p=timeline).

Financial Stability Board. 2012. "Global Shadow Banking Monitoring Report 2012" (18 November).

Fischer, Stanley. 1998. "Capital Account Liberalization and the Role of the IMF." In *Should the IMF Pursue Capital-Account Convertibility? Princeton: Princeton University, Essays in International Finance No. 207*. Princeton, NJ: Princeton University Press.

Fischhoff, B., P. Slovic, and S. Lichtenstein. 1977. "Knowing with Certainty: The Appropriateness of Extreme Confidence." *Journal of Experimental Psychology. Human Perception and Performance*, vol. 3, no. 4 (November):552–564.

Fisher, Irving. 1926. *Prohibition at Its Worst*. New York: The Macmillan Company.

———. 1933. "The Debt-Deflation Theory of Great Depressions." *Econometrica*, vol. 1, no. 4 (October):337–357.

Flood, R.P., and P.M. Garber. 1984. "Collapsing Exchange-Rate Regimes: Some Linear Examples." *Journal of International Economics*, vol. 17, no. 1–2:1–13.

Fontaine, J.S., and R. Garcia. 2012. "Bond Liquidity Premia." *Review of Financial Studies*, vol. 25, no. 4 (April):1207–1254.

Fontaine, J.S., R. Garcia, and S. Gungor. 2013. "Funding Liquidity Risk and the Cross-Section of Stock Returns" (February): www.banque-france.fr/fondation/gb/telechar/pdf/paper-garcia-2013-04-19.pdf.

Forbes, Kristin. 2012. "'Capital Controls: Gates versus Walls': Comments and Discussion." *Brookings Papers on Economic Activity*, Fall:356–363.

Forbes, Kristin, Marcel Fratzscher, Thomas Kostka, and Roland Straub. 2012. "Bubble Thy Neighbor: Portfolio Effects and Externalities from Capital Controls." NBER Working Paper 18052 (May).

Friedman, Milton. 2007. "An Interview with Milton Friedman. Interviewed by John B. Taylor, May 2000." In *Inside the Economist's Mind. Conversations with Eminent Economists*. Edited by P. Samuelson and W. Barnett. Oxford, UK: Blackwell.

Galati, Gabriele, and Richhild Moessner. 2011. "Macroprudential Policy—A Literature Review." BIS Working Paper 337 (February): www.bis.org/publ/work337.pdf.

Gallagher, Kevin P. 2012. "Regaining Control: Capital Controls and the Global Financial Crisis." In *The Consequences of the Global Financial Crisis: The Rhetoric of Reform and Regulation*. Edited by Wyn Grant and Graham Wilson. Oxford, UK: Oxford University Press.

Gertler, Mark. 1994. "Financial Conditions and Macroeconomic Behavior." *NBER Reporter* (Summer): 10–14.

Gorton, Gary B. 2010. *Slapped by the Invisible Hand: The Panic of 2007*. New York: Oxford University Press.

Gorton, Gary, and Andrew Metrick. 2010. "Securitized Banking and the Run on Repo." Yale ICF Working Paper 09-14.

Greenwood, Robin, and Samuel G. Hanson. 2013. "Issuer Quality and Corporate Bond Returns." *Review of Financial Studies*, vol. 26, no. 6 (June):1483–1525.

Gromb, Denis, and Dimitri Vayanos. 2002. "Equilibrium and Welfare in Markets with Financially Constrained Arbitrageurs." *Journal of Financial Economics*, vol. 66, no. 2–3 (November–December):361–407.

Grossman, Sanford J., and Merton H. Miller. 1988. "Liquidity and Market Structure." *Journal of Finance*, vol. 43, no. 3 (July):617–633.

Haldane, Andrew G. 2012. "On Being the Right Size." Speech given at the Institute of Economic Affairs' 22nd Annual Series, the 2012 Beesley Lectures at the Institute of Directors (25 October): www.bankofengland.co.uk/publications/Documents/speeches/2012/speech615.pdf.

Hall, Robert E. 2010. "Why Does the Economy Fall to Pieces after a Financial Crisis?" *Journal of Economic Perspectives*, vol. 24, no. 4 (Fall):3–20 http://pubs.aeaweb.org/doi/pdfplus/10.1257/jep.24.4.3.

Hansen, Lars Peter. 2013. "Challenges in Identifying and Measuring Systemic Risk" (14 February): www.larspeterhansen.org/documents/FC_2012_Risk_BookSRMM_Challenges_in_Identifying.pdf.

Hasbrouck, Joel. 2006. "Trading Costs and Returns for US Equities: Estimating Effective Costs from Daily Data." Working paper, New York University (August): http://pages.stern.nyu.edu/~jhasbrou/Research/GibbsEstimates2006/ctc10.pdf.

Hausmann, Ricardo, and Ugo Panizza. 2003. "The Determinants of Original Sin: An Empirical Investigation." *Journal of International Money and Finance*, vol. 22, no. 7 (December):957–990.

Hayek, F.A. 1933. "Monetary Policy and the Trade Cycle."

He, Zhiguo, and Arvind Krishnamurthy. 2012. "A Model of Capital and Crises, 2012." *Review of Economic Studies*, vol. 79, no. 2 (April):735–777.

———. 2013. "Intermediary Asset Pricing." *American Economic Review*, vol. 103, no. 2 (April):732–770.

Hicks, J.R. 1937. "Mr. Keynes and the "Classics"; A Suggested Interpretation." *Econometrica*, vol. 5, no. 2 (April):147–159.

Hoshi, Takeo, and A. Kashyap. 2010. "Will the U.S. Bank Recapitalization Succeed? Eight Lessons from Japan." *Journal of Financial Economics*, vol. 97, no. 3 (September):398–417.

———. 2013. *What Stopped Japan's Economic Growth? Prescriptions for the Revival (Nani ga Nihon no Seicho wo Tometanoka—Saisei he no Shohosen)*. Tokyo: Nihon Keizai Shimbun.

Ibbotson, Roger G., Jeffrey J. Diermeier, and Laurence B. Siegel. 1984. "The Demand for Capital Market Returns: A New Equilibrium Theory." *Financial Analysts Journal*, vol. 40, no. 1 (January/February):22–33.

IMF. 2008. *World Economic Outlook, April 2008: Housing and the Business Cycle.* Washington, DC: International Monetary Fund (www.imf.org/external/pubs/ft/weo/2008/01).

―――. 2010. *World Economic Outlook, April 2010: Rebalancing Growth.* Washington, DC: International Monetary Fund (www.imf.org/external/pubs/ft/weo/2010/01).

―――. 2011a. "IMF Performance in the Run-Up to the Financial and Economic Crisis: IMF Surveillance in 2004–07." Independent Evaluation Office of the International Monetary Fund (10 January): www.elpais.com/elpaismedia/ultimahora/media/201102/09/economia/20110209elpepueco_2_Pes_PDF.pdf.

―――. 2011b. "IMF Develops Framework to Manage Capital Inflows." *IMF Survey Magazine* (5 April): www.imf.org/External/pubs/ft/survey/so/2011/NEW040511B.htm.

―――. 2012. "The Liberalization and Management of Capital Flows: An Institutional View." Policy paper (14 November): www.imf.org/external/np/pp/eng/2012/111412.pdf.

Jeanne, Olivier. 2012. "Capital Account Policies and the Real Exchange Rate." NBER Working Paper 18404 (September): www.nber.org/papers/w18404.

Jeanne, Olivier, and Anton Korinek. 2013. "Macroprudential Regulation versus Mopping Up after the Crash." NBER Working Paper 18675 (December): www.nber.org/papers/w18675.

―――. 2014. "Macroprudential Policy Beyond Banking Regulation," *Financial Stability Review* (Banque de France), no. 18 (April): 163–172.

Jonung, Lars, and Eoin Drea. 2009. "The Euro: It Can't Happen. It's a Bad Idea. It Won't Last. US Economists on the EMU, 1989–2002." European Commission Economic Paper 395 (December): http://ec.europa.eu/economy_finance/publications/publication16345_en.pdf.

Kacperczyk, Marcin, and Philipp Schnabl. 2013. "How Safe Are Money Market Funds?" *Quarterly Journal of Economics*, vol. 128, no. 3 (August):1073–1122.

Keynes, John Maynard. 1936. *The General Theory of Employment, Interest, and Money.* London: Macmillan and Co.

Kindleberger, C. 2000. *Manias, Panics and Crashes.* 4th ed. Hoboken, NJ: John Wiley & Sons.

Kinlaw, Will, Mark Kritzman, and David Turkington. 2012. "Toward Determining Systemic Importance." *Journal of Portfolio Management*, vol. 38, no. 4 (Summer):100–111.

Kiyotaki, N., and J. Moore. 1997. "Credit Cycles." *Journal of Political Economy*, vol. 105, no. 2 (April):211–248.

Klein, Michael W. 2012. "Capital Controls: Gates versus Walls." *Brookings Papers on Economic Activity*, Fall:317–355.

Kocherlakota, Narayana R. 2000. "Creating Business Cycles through Credit Constraints." *Federal Reserve Bank of Minneapolis Quarterly Review*, vol. 24, no. 3 (Summer):2–10 (www.minneapolisfed.org/research/qr/qr2431.pdf).

Kodres, Laura. 2012. "Not Making the Grade: Report Card on Global Financial Reform." *iMFdirect* (28 September).

Koo, Richard. 2013. "Central Banks in Balance Sheet Recessions: A Search for Correct Response." Nomura Research Institute (31 March). http://snbchf.snbchfcom.netdna-cdn.com/wp-content/uploads/2013/04/Koo-Ineffectiveness-Monetary-Expansion.pdf

Korinek, Anton. 2010. "Regulating Capital Flows: Design and Implementation Issues." VoxEU (22 December).

———. 2011a. "The New Economics of Prudential Capital Controls: A Research Agenda." *IMF Economic Review*, vol. 59, no. 3 (August):523–561.

———. 2011b. "Risk-Taking: Amplification Effects, Externalities, and Regulatory Responses." ECB Working Paper 1345 (June).

Korinek, Anton, and Enrique Mendoza. 2013. "From Sudden Stop to Fisherian Deflation: Quantitative Theory and Policy Implications." NBER Working Paper 19362 (August).

Kouparitsas, Michael A. 2001. "Is the United States an Optimum Currency Area? An Empirical Analysis of Regional Business Cycles." Federal Reserve Bank of Chicago Working Paper 2001-22 (December).

Krishnamurthy, Arvind, Stefan Nagel, and Dmitry Orlov. Forthcoming. "Sizing Up Repo." *Journal of Finance*.

Kritzman, Mark P. 2012. "Toward Determining Systemic Importance." Presentation at the Q Group seminar in Wesley Chapel, FL (3 April).

Krugman, Paul. 1979. "A Model of Balance-of-Payments Crises." *Journal of Money, Credit and Banking*, vol. 11, no. 3 (August):311–325.

———. 2009. "How Did Economists Get It So Wrong?" *New York Times Magazine* (2 September): www.nytimes.com/2009/09/06/magazine/06Economic-t.html?pagewanted=all.

———. 2011. "Mr Keynes and the Moderns." VoxEu (21 June): www.voxeu.org/article/mr-keynes-and-moderns.

———. 2013. "Currency Regimes, Capital Flows, and Crises." Paper presented at 14th Jacques Polak Annual Research Conference at the IMF (www.imf.org/external/np/res/seminars/2013/arc/pdf/krugman.pdf).

Lapavitsas, Costas. 2012. *Crisis in the Eurozone*. London: Verso.

Leijonhufvud, Axel. 1968. *On Keynesian Economics and the Economics of Keynes: A Study in Monetary Theory*. London: Oxford University Press.

Leijonhufvud, Axel. 2009. "Out of the Corridor: Keynes and the Crisis." *Cambridge Journal of Economics*, vol. 33, no. 4 (July):741–757.

Lou, Xiaoxia, and Ronnie Sadka. 2011. "Liquidity Level or Liquidity Risk? Evidence from the Financial Crisis." *Financial Analysts Journal*, vol. 67, no. 3 (May/June):51–62.

Lucas Jr, Robert. 1978. "Asset Prices in an Exchange Economy." *Econometrica*, vol. 46, no. 6 (November):1429–1445.

———. 2003. "Macroeconomic Priorities." Presidential address delivered at the 115th meeting of the American Economic Association (4 January): http://pages.stern.nyu.edu/~dbackus/Taxes/Lucas%20priorities%20AER%2003.pdf.

McCloskey, Deirdre. 2005. "The Trouble with Mathematics and Statistics in Economics." *History of Economic Ideas*, vol. 13, no. 3:85–102.

———. 1994. *Knowledge and Persuasion in Economics*. Cambridge University Press.

McCulley, Paul. 2009. "The Shadow Banking System and Hyman Minsky's Economic Journey." PIMCO (May): http://media.pimco.com/Documents/GCB%20Focus%20May%2009.pdf.

Mehrling, Perry. 2000. "Minsky and Modern Finance." *Journal of Portfolio Management*, vol. 26, no. 2 (Winter):81–88.

———. 2011. "The Inherent Instability of Credit." Institute for New Economic Thinking (3 March): http://ineteconomics.org/blog/money-view/inherent-instability-of-credit.

Mehrling, Perry, Zoltan Pozsar, James Sweeney, and Dan Neilson. 2012. "Bagehot Was a Shadow Banker: Shadow Banking, Central Banking, and the Future of Global Finance" Working paper (15 August).

Mendoza, Enrique G. 2010. "Sudden Stops, Financial Crises, and Leverage." *American Economic Review*, vol. 100, no. 5 (December):1941–1966.

Mian, Atif, and Amir Sufi. 2009. "The Consequences of Mortgage Credit Expansion: Evidence from the U.S. Mortgage Default Crisis." *Quarterly Journal of Economics*, vol. 124, no. 4 (November):1449–1496 (http://qje.oxfordjournals.org/content/124/4/1449.short).

———. 2010. "Household Leverage and the Recession of 2007–09." *IMF Economic Review*, vol. 58, no. 1 (August): 74–117.

———. 2014. *House of Debt: How They (and You) Caused the Great Recession and How We Can Prevent It from Happening Again*. Chicago: University of Chicago Press.

Mill, John Stuart. 1848. *Principles of Political Economy with Some of Their Applications to Social Philosophy*. London: Longmans, Green and Co.

Minsky, H. 1967. "Financial Intermediation in the Money and Capital Markets." In *Issues in Banking and Monetary Analysis*. Edited by G. Pontecorvo, R.P. Shay, and A.G. Hart. New York: Holt, Rinehart and Winston.

———. 1982. *Can "It" Happen Again?: Essays on Instability and Finance.* Armonk, NY: M.E. Sharpe.

Modigliani, F., and M.H. Miller. 1958. "The Cost of Capital, Corporate Finance and the Theory of Investment." *American Economic Review*, vol. 48, no. 3 (June):261–297.

Moore, Kyle, and Chen Zhou. 2014. "The Determinants of Systemic Importance LSE." SRC Discussion Paper 19 (August).

Morgenson, Gretchen, and Joshua Rosner. 2011. *Reckless Endangerment: How Outsized Ambition, Greed, and Corruption Led to the Worst Financial Crisis of Our Time.* New York: Times Books.

Mundell, Robert. 1961. "A Theory of Optimum Currency Areas." *American Economic Review*, vol. 51, no. 4 (September):657–665.

Muir, Tyler. 2014. "Financial Crises and Risk Premia." Working paper.

Myers, S. 1977. "Determinants of Corporate Borrowing." *Journal of Financial Economics*, vol. 5, no. 2 (November):147–175.

Obstfeld, M. 1994. "The Logic of Currency Crises." *Cahiers Économiques et Monétaires*, no. 43:189–213.

OECD Economics Department. 2014. "OECD Forecasts During and After the Financial Crisis: A Post Mortem." Policy Note 23 (February): www.oecd.org/eco/outlook/OECD-Forecast-post-mortem-policy-note.pdf.

OFR. 2012. "A Survey of Systemic Risk Analytics." Office of Financial Research Working Paper 001.

Peek, Joe, and Eric S. Rosengren. 2005. "Unnatural Selection: Perverse Incentives and the Misallocation of Credit in Japan." *American Economic Review*, vol. 95, no. 4 (September):1144–1166.

Pigou, Arthur C. 1949. *The Veil of Money.* London: Macmillan & Co.

Pozsar, Zoltan, Tobias Adrian, Adam Ashcraft, and Hayley Boesky. 2010. "Shadow Banking." Federal Reserve Bank of New York Staff Report 458 (July): www.newyorkfed.org/research/staff_reports/sr458.pdf.

Reinhart, C., and K. Rogoff. 2009. *This Time Is Different: Eight Centuries of Financial Folly.* Princeton, NJ: Princeton University Press.

Reis, Ricardo. 2013. "The Portuguese Slump and Crash and the Euro Crisis." *Brookings Papers on Economic Activity* (Spring): www.brookings.edu/~/media/Projects/BPEA/Spring%202013/2013a_reis.pdf.

Rey, Hélène. 2013. "Dilemma Not Trilemma: The Global Cycle and Monetary Policy Independence." *Proceedings—Economic Policy Symposium—Jackson Hole*:1–2 (www.kansascityfed.org/publicat/sympos/2013/2013Rey.pdf).

Sadka, R. 2012. "Hedge-Fund Performance." *Journal of Investment Management*, vol. 10, no. 2, special hedge fund issue (Second quarter): 60–72.

Samuelson, Paul A. 1939. "A Synthesis of the Principle of Acceleration and the Multiplier." *Journal of Political Economy*, vol. 47, no. 6 (December):786–797 (http://links.jstor.org/sici?sici=0022-3808%28193912%2947%3A6%3C786%3AASOTPO%3E2.0.CO%3B2-B).

Samuelson, Paul A. and William A. Barnett, eds. 2007. *Inside the Economist's Mind: Conversations with Eminent Economists*. Malden, MA: Blackwell Publishing.

Schmitt–Grohé, Stephanie, and Martin Uribe. 2013. "Downward Nominal Wage Rigidity and the Case for Temporary Inflation in the Eurozone." *Journal of Economic Perspectives*, vol. 27, no. 3 (Summer):193–212.

Schularick, Moritz, and Alan M. Taylor. 2009. "Credit Booms Gone Bust: Monetary Policy, Leverage Cycles, and Financial Crises, 1870–2008." NBER Working Paper 15512 (www.nber.org/papers/w15512).

Schumpeter, Joseph. 1954. *History of Economic Analysis*. New York: Oxford University Press.

Sharpe, W. 1964. "Capital Asset Prices: A Theory of Market Equilibrium under Conditions of Risk." *Journal of Finance*, vol. 19, no. 3 (September):425–442.

Siegel, Laurence B. 2008. "Alternatives and Liquidity: Will Spending and Capital Calls Eat Your 'Modern' Portfolio?" *Journal of Portfolio Management*, vol. 35, no. 1 (Fall):103–114.

Sinn, Hans-Werner. 2014. *The Euro Trap: On Bursting Bubbles, Budgets, and Beliefs*. Oxford, UK: Oxford University Press.

Stein, Jeremy C. 2014. "Incorporating Financial Stability Considerations into a Monetary Policy Framework." Speech at the International Research Forum on Monetary Policy, Washington, DC (21 March): www.federalreserve.gov/newsevents/speech/stein20140321a.htm.

Swensen, David. 2000. *Pioneering Portfolio Management: An Unconventional Approach to Institutional Investment*. New York: Free Press.

Taylor, Alan. 2012. "The Great Leveraging." NBER Working Paper 18290 (August): http://economics.ucdavis.edu/people/amtaylor/files/w18290.pdf.

Teulings, Coen, and Richard Baldwin. 2014. *Secular Stagnation: Facts, Causes, and Cures*. Vox eBook (August): www.voxeu.org/article/secular-stagnation-facts-causes-and-cures-new-vox-ebook.

Thaler, Richard. ed. 2005. *Advances in Behavioral Finance, Volume II*. Princeton, NJ: Princeton University Press.

Tobin, J. 1978. "A Proposal for International Monetary Reform." *Eastern Economic Journal*, vol. 4, no. 3–4:153–159.

Tovar, Camilo E. 2008. "DSGE Models and Central Banks." BIS Working Paper 258 (September): www.bis.org/publ/work258.pdf.

Vayanos, Dimitri, and Jiang Wang. 2012. "Theories of Liquidity." *Foundations and Trends in Finance*, vol. 6, no. 4 (November): 221–317.

White, William R. 2013. "Is Monetary Policy a Science? The Interaction of Theory and Practice Over the Last 50 Years." Federal Reserve Bank of Dallas Globalization and Monetary Policy Institute Working Paper 155 (September): www.dallasfed.org/assets/documents/institute/wpapers/2013/0155.pdf.

Wiberg, Magnus. 2013. "We Tried a Tobin Tax and It Didn't Work." *Financial Times* (15 April): www.ft.com/intl/cms/s/0/b9b40fee-9236-11e2-851f-00144feabdc0.html#axzz3DPBmzJ00.

Yale Endowment. 2010. "The Yale Endowment 2010" (www.yale.edu/investments/Yale_Endowment_10.pdf).

RESEARCH FOUNDATION CONTRIBUTION FORM

☑**Yes**, I want the Research Foundation to continue to fund innovative research that advances the investment management profession. Please accept my tax-deductible contribution at the following level:

Thought Leadership Circle................. US$1,000,000 or more
Named Endowment .... US$100,000 to US$999,999
Research Fellow .... US$10,000 to US$99,999
Contributing Donor........................ US$1,000 to US$9,999
Friend .... Up to US$999

I would like to donate $ _____ .

☐ My check is enclosed (payable to the Research Foundation of CFA Institute).

☐ I would like to donate appreciated securities (send me information).

☐ Please charge my donation to my credit card.

◼VISA ◼MC ◼Amex ◼Diners

Card Number

___/___
Expiration Date   Name on card   P L E A S E   P R I N T

☐ Corporate Card

☐ Personal Card

Signature

☐ This is a pledge. Please bill me for my donation of $ _____

☐ I would like recognition of my donation to be:

◼ Individual donation ◼ Corporate donation ◼ Different individual

PLEASE PRINT NAME OR COMPANY NAME AS YOU WOULD LIKE IT TO APPEAR

PLEASE PRINT ☐ Mr. ☐ Mrs. ☐ Ms. MEMBER NUMBER_____

Last Name (Family Name)   First   Middle Initial

Title

Address

City   State/Province   Country ZIP/Postal Code

Please mail this completed form with your contribution to:
The Research Foundation of CFA Institute • P.O. Box 2082
Charlottesville, VA 22902-2082 USA

For more on the Research Foundation of CFA Institute, please visit www.cfainstitute.org/learning/foundation/Pages/index.aspx.